Chronicles of Majnun Layla and Selected Poems

Middle East Literature in Translation
Michael Beard *and* Adnan Haydar, *Series Editors*

KING FAHD CENTER FOR
MIDDLE EAST STUDIES

TRANSLATION OF ARABIC LITERATURE
2013 AWARD WINNER

Syracuse University Press and the King Fahd Center for Middle East and Islamic Studies, University of Arkansas, are pleased to announce CHRONICLES OF MAJNUN LAYLA AND SELECTED POEMS *as the 2013 winner of the King Fahd Center for Middle East Studies Translation of Arabic Literature Award.*

Previous winners of the *King Fahd Center* prize

Blood Test: A Novel
   Abbas Beydoun; Max Weiss, trans.

The Pistachio Seller
   Reem Bassiouney; Osman Nusairi, trans.

Tree of Pearls, Queen of Egypt
   Jurji Zaydan; Samah Selim, trans.

The World Through the Eyes of Angels
   Mahmoud Saeed; Samuel Salter, Zahra Jishi,
   and Rafah Abuinnab, trans.

CHRONICLES OF
MAJNUN LAYLA
AND SELECTED POEMS

Qassim Haddad

Translated by Ferial Ghazoul and John Verlenden

Syracuse University Press

English translation copyright © 2014 Ferial Ghazoul and John Verlenden
Syracuse, New York 13244-5290

First Edition 2014
14 15 16 17 18 19   6 5 4 3 2 1

∞ The paper used in this publication meets the minimum requirements of the American National Standard for Information Sciences—Permanence of Paper for Printed Library Materials, ANSI Z39.48-1992.

For a listing of books published and distributed by Syracuse University Press, visit www.SyracuseUniversityPress.syr.edu.

ISBN: 978-0-8156-1037-3 (paper)   978-0-8156-5288-5 (e-book)

Library of Congress Cataloging-in-Publication Data
Haddad, Qasim.
  [Poems. Selections. English]
  Chronicles of Majnun Layla and selected poems / Qassim Haddad ;
translated by Ferial Ghazoul and John Verlenden. — First edition.
      pages cm — (Middle East literature in translation)
  Includes bibliographical references.
  ISBN 978-0-8156-1037-3 (pbk. : alk. paper) — ISBN 978-0-8156-5288-5 (e-book)
1. Haddad, Qasim—Translations into English.   I. Ghazoul, Ferial Jabouri,
1939– translator.   II. Verlenden, John, 1947– translator.   III. Title.
  PJ7828.D235A2 2014
  892.7'16—dc23   2014023776

Manufactured in the United States of America

The Writer is not enslaved by forms; he creates and betrays forms simultaneously.

—Qassim Haddad

The work of **Qassim Haddad** (born 1948, Bahrain) embodies the innovative trends in Arabic poetry since World War II. His vision and language, while exploring Arab heritage, are committed to a progressive perspective. He has published more than twenty collections of poetry and prose.

Ferial Ghazoul is a critic, translator, and professor and chair of the Department of English and Comparative Literature at the American University in Cairo. She is the editor of the trilingual annual *Alif: Journal of Comparative Poetics*. She has published extensively on medieval and postcolonial literatures.

John Verlenden has literary degrees from Rhodes College and Louisiana State University. He taught as a Fulbright scholar in Jordan in 1999–2000 and began teaching at American University in Cairo in 1993. His poetry, fiction, and nonfiction appear in journals.

CONTENTS

Acknowledgments

Thanks go to Walid El Hamamsy for his expert readings and textual suggestions of both Arabic and English in several lengthy passages. Thanks also to As'ad Khairallah, an authority on Majnun Layla, for his help and suggestions; the poet Qassim Haddad for responding to questions related to his poems; Adnan Haydar for his encouragement; and Neil Hewison for his moral support. Our appreciation also goes to the anonymous judges of the University of Arkansas Arabic Translation Award for 2013, who read our translation and commented on it, and to artist Dia Azzawi, whose illustration of Majnun Layla is used for the cover. Thanks to Jorge Vallery Verlenden and Nicholas Hopkins for lending their patient ears and critical comments during two years of translation. Finally, special thanks to Omneya Ali for her custodianship of the manuscript in its many different drafts, as well as her general administrative skill in processing and archiving grant documents.

Some poems in this collection appeared, sometimes in slightly different form, in *Banipal*, *Al-Ahram Weekly*, and *Al-Kalimah*.

The Qassim Haddad Translation Project has been made possible in part by a major grant from the National Endowment for the Humanities: Exploring the human endeavor.

NOTE ON·TRANSLATION

O ur translation approach is eclectic but hierarchical among its various orientations. While we initially locate the literal meaning of the Arabic in English, the nature of poetry—and good prose—demands that any other possible meanings be also noted and studied with an eye to teasing out subtextual motifs, linguistic tropes, and themes. Accordingly, literal meaning and secondary and tertiary meanings—and more, if the translators espy them—make up the initial level of concern. However, the aura, the evanescent and otherwise nonliteral feel of the text, is the greater concern, and, if necessary, the literal level must be subjugated in order for tonality (which also expresses a level of theme) and for the larger sense of the poetry's music to continue to develop a harmonious whole. In other words, sound and sense (built upon literal meaning) are considered simultaneously.

Concretely speaking, every verse line posed a plethora of choices for the co-translators in which negotiation of meaning as well as poetic effect had to be balanced. Our objective has always been to carry over the diverse tones and the poetic ambiguities of the Arabic; aware that all translations are *ijtihad*, a performance in the target language of a text from a source language based on an informed and laborious interpretation of the original. However, in the case of Haddad's collection of Majnun Layla, the different versions—poetic renderings and historical accounts of the classic love story—were both embedded and subverted. The title of the collection of Haddad's *Akhbar Majnun Layla* was a challenge. Should we keep it as Majnun Layla (which can be confusing because there are so many versions of the legend), or should we try to translate *Akhbar* (plural of *khabar*)? *Khabar*, itself, is a specific subgenre in Arabic narration that ranges in meaning from an anecdote to a historical account, from a news item to a reliable report. *Khabar* is as culturally specific as haiku and sonnet are to East Asia and Europe. In the end, we decided to translate it to "chronicles" as the term has the aura of premodern historical accounts, of events of times past—often mixed with legendary motifs—related in bits and pieces, in fragments, rather than cohering into an organic history as we understand it today. A title such as "Narratives of Majnun Layla" would have been rather flat as well as emphasizing a collection of narrated incidents. "Story" or "Stories of Majnun Layla" would have emphasized the fictional aspect of the classic love story, while Haddad wanted to use historical accounts in order to discredit their unquestioned validity. In presenting and deconstructing the different *akhbar* about Majnun, Haddad indicates that each has his own Majnun and he—as an author and a poet—has the right to construct his Majnun as he merges poetically and aesthetically with him. The Arabic word Majnun is fairly well recognized in various cultural settings, thanks to the circulation of the plot and its protagonists in Asia and Europe. Thus using Majnun Layla in the title would be understood to anyone who has a cursory knowledge of world classics. Majnun does not simply mean for non-Arab speakers a madman but someone who is driven to madness by unrequited love. Its use in its transliterated spelling evokes the Other and the passionate Other at that.

In our translation, we aspired to preserve the unfamiliar while producing a certain recognition of it, feeling at home with its strangeness. Freud called this tendency *das Unheimliche*, the uncanny. It is as if we are both confronted with the strangeness of a situation but deep inside realize its mirroring of our depths. In the first poem "Of Qays" in *Chronicles of Majnun Layla*, Haddad establishes his identification with Majnun. It opens with *sa-aqulu*, literally "I will say," and then moves on to Haddad's poetic mask, Qays. "I will say" not only lacks lyricism in English but sounds as if one is about to make a pronouncement or a commandment. The trilateral root of the Arabic verb, however, has produced the term *qawwal*, indicating an itinerant singer or poet—all of which would be echoed for an Arabic-speaking reader but is lost in translation. In the Arabic poem, the statement works as refrain in the opening of the four stanzas. It announces the lyrical narration of Majnun's life and love and thus carries in it the oral aspect of a *rawi* (reciter) of poems of others. Both the lyrical and the oral are better captured by "I sing of," which conjures the bard and the reciter declaiming while surrounded by seated audience.

Arabic syntactical structures are dissimilar from English ones. The emphatic is often used through repetition as in *al-mafʿul al-mutlaq* (the unrestricted object) such as "baka li al-buka". This does not work in English as one cannot say "wept the weeping for me." The Arabic emphasizes the enormity of grief and weeping in this recognized format, so we rendered it as "went on weeping." Here the repetition is not of the same trilateral root *baka* (wept) as in the Arabic, but repetition resides in the visual and aural alliteration of the letters and sound of *we-* in "went" and "weeping."

We strived for the poetic impact not only in the use of words, syntax, and punctuation but in the silences of the text and in the layout of the poem. Haddad writes his poems in poetic prose as well as in verse and as epigrams. While respecting his stanzas and verse lines, occasionally we used our aesthetic judgment in breaking lines or joining them, in leaving spaces between words or italicizing them. Explanatory notes (located after the appendix) explain some of the culturally specific concepts or objects, thus avoiding interruptive footnotes on the poem page. In an effort to provide the reader with the pleasure of individual reading and discovery, we abstained from explicit interpretations. But in order not to be lost in the intertextual labyrinth, we offered a general introduction situating the poet and contextualizing his poetics.

Since the translation is essentially meant for English-speaking readers, we used a simplified form of the standard transliteration system whenever we referred to an Arabic word or name in English spelling, while keeping the diacritical marks to the minimum. Names of contemporary authors mentioned in the book are written as they spell them in English. For the bilingual reader, we provided the page numbers and the source of each poem.

Chronicles of Majnun Layla and Selected Poems

INTRODUCTION

B ahrain is a small island state in the Arabian Gulf, east of
Saudi Arabia, that has witnessed radical changes in the last
fifty years or so, having moved from traditional lifestyles to mod-
ern ones. No one has captured these drastic transformations
and lived them out as expressively as the Bahraini poet Qassim
Haddad. As a child, he partook of traditional Gulf Arab life and
grew up to educate himself, thanks to his position as a librarian
and to his autodidactic impulse. Perhaps as a result of educating
himself, Haddad assimilated a contemporary outlook, adapting
his traditional vision to modern modes and beyond—to discov-
ering his own perspectives—without sacrificing local setting or
erasing past legacies. The archeological heritage of Bahrain (lit-
erally, "Two Seas") relates to the ancient civilizations of Meso-
potamia. Bahrain was once known as Dalmun, meaning "Land
of Immortality," probably because Utnapishtim, the immortal in
Sumerian mythology, lived there; and it is mentioned in the first
extant literary work of humanity, *The Epic of Gilgamesh*.

Qassim Haddad's Background

Qassim's family name "Haddad," which means literally "black-
smith," comes from the profession of his father who became a
blacksmith after working as a pearl diver—the dangerous and
typical profession of the people of Bahrain before the discovery of

oil.[1] As a child, young Qassim helped his father in his work and developed a mastery of techniques in forging and fashioning iron and other metals.

Haddad was born in 1948 in Muharraq—"the source of life in Bahrain" as he put it in an interview.[2] He spent the first decade of his life there before modernization swept away traditional life, leaving "an unannounced nostalgia for a world that is no more," as he refers to it in his memoir.[3] In his early childhood, Muharraq—located between sea and desert—was a close-knit community. In the popular neighborhoods, doors of different households were open to anyone and all. His own house was the locus of many crosscurrents: social, religious, and economic. The women of his household performed the socioreligious rite of Husayniyya where the martyrdom of Husayn, grandson of Prophet Muhammad, in Karbala in 680, is ritually retold in an elegiac mode—reminiscent of the Passion of Christ on Good Friday. Adherents of various religious orientations frequented the house. The men in the family, as pearl divers and craftsmen, had contact with other craftsmen and middlemen who traveled in the Gulf—all of whom visited the family. It is in the midst of this openness and multiplicity of professions, faiths, and social groupings that young Qassim grew up, partaking in the heterogeneous world of his community and feeling at home with diversity.

1. For a comprehensive article on pearl diving in Bahrain outlining techniques and economy, see Ahmad Humaidan, "Sayd al-lu'lu' fi al-Bahrain" [Pearl Hunting in Bahrain], *Al-Bahrain al-Thaqafiyya* 22 (October 1999): 110–22.

2. Qassim Haddad, *Fitnat al-Su'wal: Hiwarat* [The Incitement of Question: Interviews], edited by Sayyid Mahmoud (Beirut: Al-Mu'sasa al-'Arabiyya lil-Dirasat wal-Nashr, 2008): 318.

3. Qassim Haddad, *Warshat al-Amal: Sira Shakhsiyya li-Madinat al-Muharraq* [The Workshop of Hope: A Personal Biography of Muharraq City] (Bahrain: Markaz al-Shaykh Ibrahim Al Khalifa, 2004): 9.

Qassim joined *al-kuttab*, the religious preschool to which children are sent before they enroll in formal schooling. What might be significant in this experience is that his first teacher in the *kuttab* was a woman who supervised the children in memorizing verses from the Quran as she carried out household tasks. Only later did Qassim have a male instructor, so his experience of the sacred was not exclusively marked by masculinity. Similarly, while he often heard his father reciting the Quran, particularly during Ramadan, he also heard his aunts chanting the Husayniyya. Qassim was not given to the culture of memorization prevalent then but was deeply touched when listening to the charged rhythms around him.[4] Later he attended formal schools, which broadened his horizons to the contemporary world.

Qassim did not feel at ease with the restrictions of formal instruction and dropped out of secondary school to join the national library as a staff member (1968–1975). This position offered him a variety of reading material, and he explored it passionately. As a youthful Bahraini, he was impatient with the political system and its restrictions at a time when the Left and pan-Arab nationalists were trying to go beyond what they perceived to be the narrow confines of statehood and, more locally, beyond the personal interests of a dominant class. He was a political activist and paid for his convictions by being imprisoned for five years, just at the time when he was responsible for a family of his own.

Qassim devoted himself to cultural activism, opening new vistas for Bahraini arts and culture. In 1969, he participated in

4. Haddad grew up on rhythms that were not only religious but included other kinds of music from songs of pearl divers to wedding songs. For religious chants, work songs, and festival music, see Poul Rovsing Olsen, *Music in Bahrain: Traditional Music of the Arabian Gulf* (Moesgaard, Denmark: Jutland Archaeological Society, 2002).

founding the Bahrain Writers Association and played a pivotal role in it. In 1970, he co-founded Awal theatre in Bahrain. In 1980, he became involved in literary journalism, writing a weekly column. He became the editor of the journal *Kalimat* in 1987 and started a website on poetry called *Jihat al-Shi'r* (Poetry Direction) in the 1990s.

Qassim Haddad's Poetics

In 2001, Haddad received the prestigious prize of poetry awarded by the Owais Foundation for distinguished life achievement. He has published more than a dozen collections of poetry and works of critical prose, interviews, and a memoir, becoming an agent of literary innovation as a poet and an initiator of literary platforms. Arguably the best poet in the Arabian Gulf and one of the best in the Arab world, he has participated in conferences and poetry festivals in the Arab world, Europe, and the United States.

The poetry of Haddad evolved from political mobilization in his poetry of the 1970s, in which he used commonly circulating symbols, to more speculative and allusive poetry at the turn of the century, creating a more personal language of captivating ambiguity.[5] Given his trajectory from traditional roots to global horizons, it is not surprising to find his works integrating classical themes with modern perspectives, local motifs with world literature, and new interpretation of past legends. This is particularly evident in his rendering of the story of Majnun Layla in a collection published in 1996. He revived this classical work of

5. On the transformation of the poetics and stylistics of Haddad, see Yair Huri, "'The Queen Who Serves the Slaves': From Politics to Metapoetics in the Poetry of Qasim Haddad," *Journal of Arabic Literature* 34, no. 3 (2003): 252–79. See also Mojeb Zahrani's study, "Qassim Haddad: Sha'ir al-tajrib al-naw'i wal-lugha al-mushi'a" [Qassim Haddad: Poet of Quality Experimentation and Luminous Language], unpublished manuscript.

Arabian love and liberated it from its puritanical dimension and tribal overtones.

The selected poems translated here are meant to give a chronological sense of the development of Qassim Haddad's stylistics over four decades of poetic creativity, from his first collection published in 1970 to the recent collection published in 2009. The poem entitled "He Was Told: O Muhammad"—appearing in a collection published at the turn of the century—is drawn from a personal and moving childhood experience that is related in his memoir (chapter 15), which is translated and attached as an appendix to give the reader a glimpse of a prose account of an incident in his life that was later composed as a poem. The poem captures how time past is recalled via artful rearrangement of intimate, verbatim dialogue. The early poetry—some of it written when the poet was incarcerated—is provocative and forceful, though not didactic. The poems are, however, engaging, and the titles of the collections are indicative: *Al-Bishara* (The Annunciation; 1970), *Khuruj Ra's al-Husayn min al-Mudun al-Kha'ina* (Exit of Husayn's Head from Treasonous Cities; 1972), and *Al-Damm al-Thani* (Second Blood; 1975). Even in these early collections where Haddad rejects the complicity of Arab regimes, his allusions go beyond the Arab world. Scheherazade and Sisyphus, Che Guevara and Palestinian freedom fighters are juxtaposed, giving his poems with their references to local children's games and Bahraini pearl-diving boats a horizon that goes beyond the regional. Dreaming of a new dawn, he writes engagingly of children, agents of the future. In the first poem of this selection, "In the Eye of the Sun," Haddad apostrophizes the sun child who will embrace tomorrow. The sun is a leitmotif in the poetic work of Haddad; it represents the end of the night of suffering, ushering in a new day. In his fourth collection, *Qalb al-Hubb* (The Core of Love; 1980), one detects a drifting away from the urgency of political events to a reflective musing amid sensual evocations. In the poem entitled "Anti al-Musiqa wa-Ana al-Raqs" (You are the Music and I am the Dance), he questions the distinctions between the mover and the moved. The Syrian critic Subhi Hadidi sums up Haddad's poetic trajectory as starting in harmony with the visual recollections of the reader and then moving to a poetics that unsettles imaginative norms, leading the reader to freshly constructed poetic collages. He writes that Haddad's poetic text runs "against the current" and quotes him in one of his poems where the poetic persona asserts,

> My voice is for a river
> that runs against the norms of water
> for letters that stand against dictionaries,
> grammar and syntax
> for poetry in prose.[6]

Thus the reader of Haddad cannot count on a packaged perspective of the universe but must come prepared for a poetic surprise if not a shock, for defamiliarization of the familiar and the quotidian.

Haddad's stylistics dropped classical prosody—based on the rigid constraints of meters and monorhymes—and in this he partook in the poetic revolution of Arabic verse that was initiated in Baghdad in the late 1940s and soon spread to the rest of the Arab world in what came to be known as *taf'ila* (metric foot) poetry, or free verse. He also moved further in liberating himself from prosody by writing prose poems. At times he mixes free verse with poetic prose, and at other times he uses a pronounced rhyme scheme. Qassim Haddad is restless when it comes to poetic form. He is experimental in poetic genres too: He writes narrative

---

6. Subhi Hadidi. *Muqaddima* [Introduction]. Qassim Haddad, *Al-A'mal al-Shi'riyya* I (Beirut: Al-Mu'sasa al-'Arabiyya lil-Dirasat wal-Nashr, 2000): 30–31.

poems as well as very short, haiku-like poems. We have selected a number of his flash poems from "Catalog of Suffering," which show the effect of poetic aphorisms that align him with the writing of such medieval Sufis as al-Nifarri.

Of the more narrative poems, we selected to translate Haddad's magnificent rendering of the legend of *Majnun Layla*. Despite its wide dissemination in world literature and the arts, Haddad feels free to reinterpret the story imaginatively as well as historically. The resulting poem develops a view of the two lovers that departs from its traditional, Platonic cast. Instead, Haddad's Qays and Layla participate in an erotic plot that presents their earthly love as physical and emotional, breaking away from tribal convention. The Saudi Arabian critic Mojeb Zaharani shows in his analysis of Haddad's *Akhbar Majnun Layla* that the poet, in writing a biography of the mythical Qays, lover and poet—judged to be a madman by tribal conventions—is simultaneously writing a testimonial about himself.[7] This merging of Qays with Qassim is proclaimed by the poet in the first poem of the collection where the alliteration in the names overdetermines the announced connection.

Majnun Layla: A Traveling Classic

In the traditional telling of the story, Qays of the tribe of Banu 'Amir of Arabia became known as Majnun (madman) because his infatuation with Layla, his cousin, led him to insanity. Not permitted to wed her as he had violated patriarchal and tribal conventions by making his love known through his poetry, he roamed the wilderness until his death. Over time, Qays became synonymous

7. Mojeb Zahrani, "Lu'bat al-mahu wal-tashkil fi *Akhbar Majnun Layla*" [The Game of Erasing and Forming in the Chronicles of Majnun Layla], *Fusul* 16, no. 1 (Summer 1997): 227.

with the martyr of love, with the pining lover—devoted yet unful-filled. Partly historical and partly mythical, the figure of Qays and his beloved Layla have been recorded in chronicles in different variants, first by literary historians and later by poets of differ-ent tongues. This perennial love story has been admired, retold, and adapted in different ages and cultures since its inception in the late seventh century. It has been rendered in Persian, Turk-ish, various Indian languages, modern Arabic, and in English and French. Critics and comparativists have written about different versions of the literary manifestations of the legend.[8] Miniature painters and singers in the East and the West have represented the story. Each writer, singer, or artist emphasized an aspect of love seen in the story and adjusted it to the ethos of the context and the genre. From being a narrative about unfulfilled pasto-ral love in a tribal setting, it has been retold in an urban milieu, adding to the protagonists a more sophisticated and metropolitan characterization. From a story of human love for an inaccessible woman, the narrative has been turned into an allegory, standing for the mystic yearning to unite with the Divine. More political and autobiographical dimensions have mingled with the Majnun story in modern Arabic and French renderings.

The earliest extant account of the story of Majnun Layla was reported in the ninth century by Ibn Qutaiba (828–889) in his book *Kitab al-Shi'r wal-Shu'ara'* (The Book of Poetry and Poets).

---

8. For a thorough study of the Majnun legend, see As'ad Khairallah, *Love, Madness, and Poetry: An Interpretation of Magnun Legend* (Beirut: Orient-Insitut, 1980), where the author compares the Arabian version(s) to Jami's. On the love of Majnun, see André Miquel and Percy Kemp, *Majnun et Layla: L'amour fou* (Paris: Éditions Sindbad, 1984). For comparative studies, see (besides Khairallah's book) André Miquel, *Deux histoires d'amour: De Majnun à Tristan* (Paris: Éditions Odile Jacob, 1996) and Ali Asghar Seyed-Gohrab, *Layli and Majnun: Love, Madness, and Mystic Longing in Nizami's Epic Romance* (Leiden: Brill, 2003).

Another and a more elaborate variant of the story of Majnun Layla is narrated by Abu al-Faraj al-Asfahani (897–967) in his book *Kitab al-Aghani* (The Book of Songs). Al-Walibi, an enigmatic figure who is difficult to anchor historically, collected the poetry of Majnun Layla. The story became an exemplary narrative of intoxication with love.

As the story moved from its original setting in the desert to more urban locations, it changed in details but not in the general outline. Qays meets Layla at school in the version composed by the Persian poet Nizami (1141–1209), who succeeded in turning the story of *Layli-u-Majnun* from a series of anecdotes interspersed with poetry to a romance with an organic plot. Jami (1414–1492), influenced by Nizami and like him reversing the title of the story to become *Layla and Majnun*, gave Layla a Sufi connotation, associating her with divine beauty. Thus Majnun's longing for Layla is presented as allegorical of man's yearning for God. Jami's version intimates this by comparing the insane gestures and ravings of Majnun to those of a dancing dervish; his peaceful association with wild animals suggests the monastic desert existence of a Sufi hermit. In the conclusion of the work, Jami explains the mystic inner meaning of the story. Other authors before and after Jami adapted the legend to their worldview as in the works of the Indian Amir Khusrow Dehlawi (1253–1325) and the Azerbaijani Fuzuli (1483–1556), who again were inclined to redirect the story towards divine love. This identification of the beloved with the divine is akin to the way Dante elevated his worldly Beatrice into a quasi-holy figure in his *Divine Comedy*. In 1797, Isaac D'Israeli published *Mejnun and Leila: The Arabian Petrarch and Laura*, based on Islamic sources; however, it is also his own creative version of the romance. This English adaptation mixes prose with poetry—as the legend often does when narrated in medieval Arabic literature. Heinrich Heine used the legend of *Majnun Layla* in his dramatic work *Almansor* published in 1821. In more recent times, critics have been able to document the scholarly interest in the legend of *Majnun Layla* in Europe, which generated several creative works, notably Louis Aragon's *Le Fou d'Elsa* (1963) and André Miquel's *Laylâ, ma raison* (1984). There have been a number of adaptations of the legend in Arabic drama and poetry including those by Egyptian poets Ahmad Shawqi (1916) and Salah Abdul-Sabur (1970) and by Iraqi poetess 'Atika al-Khazraji (1954). Egyptian poet Salah Jahin adapted it as an operetta with music by Muhammad Nuh (1982).

The figures of Majnun and Layla were represented in miniatures and in paintings all over western and central Asia, and many of these art works are found today in Western museums. Folk artists have represented the lovers and their agonizing passions. Music and dance have also played their parts in diffusing the work. An operatic work based on *Majnun Layla* was composed by Uzeyir Hajibeyov and performed in Azerbaijan in 1908. A Malay film based on *Majnun Layla* was produced; Indian cinema has produced several films based on the story of *Majnun Layla*. British rock musician Eric Clapton composed a love song entitled "Layla" in 1970. Armenian American Alan Hovehaness composed in 1973 "The Majnun Symphony"; contemporary Dutch composer Rokos de Groot composed two musical works, *Majnun's Lament* and *Layla and Majnun*; Taieb Louhichi directed a Tunisian film based on Miquel's *Laylâ, ma raison* in 1989. In 2007, a ballet based on Qassim Haddad's *Akhbar Majnun Layla* was performed in Bahrain.

Qassim Haddad's *Akhbar Majnun Layla* lyrically rewrites Majnun's love story delineating its sensual dimension, which subverts tribal conventions and ideals. Haddad builds on the different historical accounts with their inconsistencies and contradictions to reimagine a modern Qays for whom the pleasures of the flesh are as important as the correspondence of the psyches. His Layla is not a helpless kept daughter but a daring, articulate woman who dismisses the worn-out customs of her people. Haddad's lyrical version of *Majnun Layla* has inspired visual artists and composers, including the Iraqi painter Dia Al-Azzawi[9] and the Lebanese composer Marcel Khalifeh. Of course, it has also received in its musical operatic rendering the wrath of conservatives and reactionaries in Bahrain's Parliament and in the Gulf media.[10]

Translation as Adventure

Translating poetry is risky. Among all the literary genres that translation can carry over to another language, poetry remains the most resistant since it is anchored in the specificity of the language. The problem is not solved by mere competence in source language and target language and possessing a bilingual poetic ear. The translation, particularly of a poem, resembles Mallarmé's window where you see through it but also you see yourself reflected in it.[11] In other words, a reader of translated poetry must be willing to play a double role: construct the indirect meaning of

9. Al-Azzawi has illustrated a special edition of Haddad's *Majnun Layla* that was printed in London by Arabesque Group in 1996. The cover painting with its rich color and composition is one of many illustrations that were specifically made for this edition by the London-based Iraqi artist Al-Azzawi.

10. On the reaction to the musical and dance rendering of Haddad's Majnun Layla, see, among others Kelly O'Brien, "Mideast Politics Put to Words and Music: Bahraini Democracy Threatened by Musical," *Al Jadid* 12, no. 56/57 (Summer/Fall 2006): 10, 18–19. See also Dalia Chams, "Deux autres fous de Laila," *Al-Ahram Hebdo* (11–17 avril): 22; and "Marcel Khalifeh wa-Qassim Haddad Yudafiʿan ʿan Majnun Layla" [Marcel Khalifeh and Qassim Haddad Defend Majnun Layla], *Al-Hayat* (March 21, 2007): 21. For a more elaborate study, see Nadra Majeed Assaf, "Dancing Without My Body: Cultural Integration in the Middle East," *Popular Culture in the Middle East and North Africa: A Postcolonial Outlook*, edited by Walid El Hamamsy and Mounira Soliman (London: Routledge, 2013): 95–109.

11. Stéphane Mallarmé, "Les fenêtres," *Oeuvres complètes* (Paris: Gallimard, 1945): 32–33.

the poem and identify with it—as one does with any poem—and also see through it the foreign allure and the seductive difference, an alterity, as Benjamin argued for.[12] The issue of problematic exchange in languages as different as Arabic and English is not only due to the different nature of the languages—a Semitic one and an Indo-European one—but also to the difference in what is called the "textual grids," the different frames of cultural reference. These grids "reflect patterns of expectations that have been interiorized by members of a given culture."[13] To overcome what is specifically local and what defies linguistic translation, in this volume explanatory notes have been provided rather than using English analogs of the concepts and material objects.

Focusing on *Akhbar Majnun Layla* as this collection's centerpiece is partly driven by the work's international dissemination, thus providing a bridge between two different textual grids. Qassim Haddad is not simply retelling the legend of Majnun: he is both evoking it and dismantling it. This work of ironic intertextuality is based on use of classical Arabic and poetry but with a modern worldview—all of which makes the translator painfully aware of the challenges. Haddad's strategy is that of a palimpsest where he does not altogether scrape off the earlier texts, but he superimposes his own on them, producing partly an erasure and partly a dialogue with the earlier text in its many variants.

Our choice has been to opt for an overt translation and not a re-creation of another original in English. The translation strives to reproduce the resistance of the original to simplified rendering

12. Walter Benjamin, "The Task of the Translator," *Theories of Translation: An Anthology from Dryden to Derrida*, edited by Rainer Schulte and John Biguenet (Chicago: University of Chicago Press, 1992): 71–82.

13. Susan Bassnett, "Culture and Translation," *A Companion to Translation Studies*, edited by Piotr Kuiwczak and Karin Littau (Clevendon, UK: Multilingual Matters, 2007): 19.

and trusts that readers will recognize in the translation a reflection of a passion that they can relate to, as well as the singularity and originality of Haddad's poetic texts. His unfamiliar syntax, strange tropes, and collage of the narrative episodes with the lyrical outpouring are precisely the stylistic specificity of the poet and also the hallmark of an undomesticated translation.

Translation is always an adventure. The translator of poetry is a seafarer in an ocean of words and tropes. We translators take risks and hope in the end that we will reach Ithaca—to borrow the metaphor of Cavafy—even if it is not the same Ithaca we left from.

CHRONICLES OF MAJNUN LAYLA

Al-'Amal al-Shi'riyya [Poetic Works]. 2 vols. Beirut: Al-Mu'sasa al-'Arabi-yya lil-Dirasat wal-Nashr, 2000. 2: 181–254.

Of Qays

I sing of Qays—
an ardor dwelling in flames,
his shaping me
in his color, name, scent
his opening and ending.
A mist primeval,
I straightened in his hands,
bore fruit.
He summoned me.
Later when he wept
complaining about me
I dispersed the crowd
—his listeners—
and considered them
never again.
In me he invested
all his pride.
His verses the people chanted yet.
So I ask: Did he ignite me
or did he choke my fire?

I sing of Qays
of a paradise
disappearing between my eyes,
of an air
making us lighter
like birds borne aloft,
choosing us.

I sing
of when he clutched me in his mind,
when I wandered in him

proud to celebrate our merging,
the rapturous love on which the Hijaz languishes,
which the Gulf shores
love in turn.

I sing of Qays
his blood-red grieving,
night pursuing his cadenced pace,
water singing his *qasida*.
He wept for me
went on weeping
prepared my howdah
stepped aside to ask the beasts
about me
as if his eye were not on the caravan
but on the half-wild horses.

I sing of Qays
of the disowned 'Amiri,
of his free-to-be-squandered blood
of a sword he unsheathed from his heart
before hurtling me across Najd to smash all arms.
Of the rare pleasures
of ecstasy, *longueurs*, nocturnal moaning
of horses neighing in me by night,
of scalding fire washing me
by morn.
O Qays
either you've driven me mad
or else it's you who's mad,
both of us night-blood
soaked in the remnants of the *qasida*.

He Is No One

He is Qays. And he is Mu'adh, son of Kulaib, and he is Qays, son of Mu'adh al-'Uqaili. Then again he is al-Buhturi, son of al-Ja'd; is al-Aqra', son of Mu'adh; also al-Mahdi. No—some said—he is the Qays who's son of al-Mulawwah from the Banu 'Amir tribe. On being queried, those clans denied it: "Not one of us. Baseless."

Then it was said he was no one really. He slogged through life with an unrequited heart—possessed. Al-Asfahani tells us—his words being based on one of the oral transmitters, a known liar whom we believed nonetheless—of a man who could apprehend the presence of invisible people. Empowered, he relates the following: "Three men are known to exist who have never existed: the son of Abu al-'Aqib, the author of the epical *qasida*; Ibn al-Qiri-yya; and Majnun of the Banu 'Amir."

As for us, it was as if we assembled the man out of paper scraps tossed away by copyists—flung on the floor then celebrated in dreams. Our native compassion, girded by imagination, revealed him to us more than any rattling storyteller could. In such a way we first heard from Abu Bakr al-Walibi, who referred us to others in the oral chain. We seized the juiciest parts of the legend: from Abu Miskin, al-Shibani, Abu Ishaq, al-Jawhari, al-Riyashi, Ibn Shabba, al-Madaini, al-Muhallabi, and al-Asma'i, who based his key work on al-Asfahani, the author of *al-Aghani*. Al-Asma'i invited us to exercise doubt; we took full advantage. We fell on whatever suited our dispositions: God led us to the truest of all the fictions. For every part taken from this or that storyteller, we celebrated with a toast. The best parts we inflated to our taste. The Majnun enjoyed it. We had a great time with him.

Of Layla

I sing of Layla,
of the honey that lounges coquettishly on the forearm,
of the lazy pomegranate,
of the *fatwa* whispering its sweet nectar simile,
of the Bedouin eyes, the fire, the cheek.

She is for me
an adventure stirring the desire of poets should they sing:
"East wind of Najd, when did you start to blow so briskly?"

Of flimsy slumber that betrays us,
of our rapturous love,
of her,
so the desert might know only aloe and laurel.

I sing of Layla,
of the slain
of our blood squandered,
of the beast-friend
and the lure of lovers,
of wakefulness seeking night
and two children timid to meet.
When the apple trees blossom
they tremble in correspondence
until timidity feels embarrassed.

Layla possesses a sweeter moan
when passion takes us astray
and flames race the length of our limbs.
Whether living or dead,
when told we've committed a sin,
a sigh will cry within us
should they forgive.

I sing of Layla,
of the traveler weeping to no end,
of the rapturous magic manifest in the message of her eyes,
of a blessing beseeching me to my end,
of her manifold mirrors stirring the desires of young men,
of her erotic scales,
of her justice in injustice,
of my travels while raving,
of a djinn selecting a slain man.

My Layla—if only her hand fall upon me.
And if my hand is consecrated
granting me the office of Messenger
then of her will I sing—if mad, songs of madness.
I have an excuse if I exaggerate
my death a little.

First Lightning

Truth, which is pure doubt, says that Qays and Layla were from the Banu 'Amir tribe. They met as child herders—in Najd of the Arabian Peninsula—in two vales connected on one side by a clutch of palms, on the other by fierce desolation.

He: disposed to premature sorrow, inclined towards solitude, often socializing with his pasturing beasts of burden, and composing for them emotional poems that people considered speeches memorized from other shepherds. He dared not claim the poetry for fear that he, a boy, would be cast as a liar. She, a dreamer, owned prolific imagination, was eccentric; her age-mates maintained she was almost entirely djinn, only partly human. She had contact with her paternal cousin and his early poetics in those two valleys where she became his mate in children's games, while growing into young manhood, his poetry becoming inflamed with her. She was captivated by him. She used to hue to the belly of the vale, so they could meet next to the brook where their sheep flocked—he with his brothers, she with her girlfriends. So they became attuned to each other. Passion flourished between them like a glow in the hearth of love. It was said that Qays narrated:

"In the creek of the two vales where we brought the sheep to drink, we would crowd the watering place with clamorous play. Each of us would get water and spray the other, we would plunge headlong at each other, our tender bodies becoming agitated. It happened that I approached her one day and my shoulder touched her breast, which was yet to perk or become round. Nevertheless, a delicate thread of lightning seared through my parts, and I saw that she quivered. Out of her mouth emerged a cry, almost a wailing, as if possessed by panic. She had happened—I knew—upon the poetry of my soul, not yet turning on my tongue. Each of us ran towards our sheep, driving them back to the campsite. For a long while, I did not see her. I did not believe I would see her, ever.

"I was close to the dream."

Not of Any Place

Doubt mingled with the biography of Majnun, causing oral transmitters to differ with regard to his poetry. Some claimed it belonged to a Banu Umayya poet who fell in love with a governor's wife. Afraid their story would become public, he attributed his verses to two names not to be found in any place. Thus the poetry circulated of Layla and her Majnun. Along the way, untruths resembling truths were added, so we believed them. Amin, author of *al-Hujra*, said in his version—without stamp or document of authority—that a man called Radwan al-Jinn claimed that Qays was real but his poetry was a fabrication, that he knew a calligrapher, Jamal al-Layl the scribe, who copied these poems. He said their composition was the act of a poet who fell in love with a young woman of the Arabian nomads who migrated between Najd and al-Ta'if. This young woman, however, was forced to marry another, so the poet, afraid of igniting fires among the tribes, took to the Peninsula's open air creating verse and legend wherever he wandered. He attributed everything to "al-Majnun"—the madman—a figure outside of blame or criticism. Thus it came to pass that whoever had quill or pen fashioned his fancies under the heading of madness. So many were these poets that no one can say there was any period lacking rhapsodic and agonizing lovers. The color-mad fell upon the poetry-mad. Flames arose on every side and heat was born anew in the blaze of memory, just as wind reddens the smoking embers.

Things

She disappeared on him; he is waiting on the roadside, his things scattered about while people pass around him like ether. Through windows in their bodies, he sees her running towards him. But she does not reach him. And he, running towards her, cannot reach her either.

Meanwhile people step over his scattered objects—a pointed sand grouse feather/a green silk thread his mother tied around his forearm when he was a child/a wedding ring worn thin from frequent removal/a talisman wrapped in hyena skin/a dry *siwak*-tree twig/a rough sapphire laced with coal/a saddlebag punctured by wind/remnants of a bridle oozing wind horses/ solitude—absorbing what their feet come across.

Women sitting next to him ask for poetry. He asks them of Layla. They say she is among them, though hiding so the tribe won't be scandalized. He says that the invisible Layla appears to him clearer than were she visible. They say, "Recite!" And he raises his voice so that she may notice him. She is there. She hears him recite verses that crush boulders while the women sigh and he laments, giving them his innermost, and the women ask for more. All the while she listens.

People pass by through cracks in their bodies, taking his dispersed things—an old turquoise stone/a pot of ambergris dregs/a child's *kufiyya* worn out by sand/a mysterious lock of hair/battle loot heaped on a saddle/anxiety—and they pass by.

Women flit about him, suffused with admiration, intrigue. He recites his poetry, they laugh with joy. He wails his lament—she listens. The women realize Qays is being taken beyond human limitations: he is close to being ruined by the silence of his beloved.

Meanwhile people pass by and his dispersed things—an empty scabbard/traces of blood on a rag holding a broken bolt/a swatch of the Quran's 'Amma yatasa'lun on yellowish paper/a love amulet/a shrunken water skin/an eagle's talon/frankincense gum/a strip of jerked meat—have almost dwindled to nothing. And she listens. The women say, "O Qays, your beloved is abusing you without mercy. Leave her! It is your right. She deserves it."

He shouts back, "By God, no! My sole concern is my unworthiness. It's her right to hear me boast of being nothing more than a thread slipped from the fringe of her belt. If she accepts it, then so do I."

Suddenly a sob from among the women: one soul is seized by a fit of weeping. The women turn to locate the source. From a corner among them a small sun rises and slides out of their midst as if through a tent door. So it is made apparent: Layla circling around them, taking away the rest of his dispersed things: a burnt stone from a three-piece desert stove/a *siwak* twig/a tuft of camel hair/a date pit pierced by horse's hair/a slipper drained of its pigmentation/sparse sleep/pale rainbow.

Qays is strung so tautly, so captivated that he can scarce control his body. Meanwhile she drifts away from him like a chemise eased off the body. He shudders: a chill wind touches his chest. Stripped now, naked to the elements. Sitting on the roadside, watering the women with poetry, he cries from thirst. They—the women—are in raptures from the love aroused in their beings, fires no moisture can smother.

The women rejoice as he weeps—his little sun moves away.

The Crystalline Sweetness of Flesh

They told Qays, "The entire desert knows of your passion for Layla—so enough of your protestations."

He said, "But Layla does not know it."

They told him, "The passion of Layla for you is the talk of the Bedouins and the city dwellers. That should be enough."

He said, "But Qays does not know it."

One night she said to him, "What I have for you is more than what you have for me. I say unto God: I shall not sit with another man until I taste death—unless I am forced to."

He spoke with her. She listened. She wept with him and ran her fingertips through the saffron of his hair until dawn readied its unveiling. She then noticed: she was the prisoner of his forearm. Strong, it contained no violence; stern, it held no harshness. She wallowed in his hard chest, her hair loosened, her gowns stripped. He was granting her what she came for, what she had never known, what had been forbidden to her.

When time caught her up, she pranced like a blazing flame. She got up drawing tight her robes as he looked for her sashes and cloak; along with her hand he tied her waistband and belt. Her things, scattered around the mats, yielded to the tent their colors of night and day—she gathered them up. She bade him farewell and left.

Thus he inherited madness by tasting her crystalline sweetness.

Now You Have Heard, Now You Have Seen

The day when the exact date of the Feast was established—so it is said—was a Tuesday, the twentieth of Dhu al-Hijja in a Hegira year when the Feast eve fell on a Friday.

On that day, more pilgrims gathered than ever before. Qays was frightened when his father, taking the advice of their people who looked to God to remove Qays's love for Layla, took him to the Kaaba. His father asked him to hang on to the drapes of that holy edifice and pray for God's relief. Qays stood on a slight elevation in the yard and yelled into the sanctuary, pilgrims milling about, "O God, may you increase my love for Layla and my devotion to her. Let me never forget her. Do nothing to distract me from her."

His father was startled. The multitudes, astonished and roused to anger, turned on Qays. They had never witnessed such a prayer in this most holy of places. They deemed it a grave business, an inadmissible godless confession, a wild wantonness that could not be ignored. They encircled Qays and seized him while he kept repeating his supplication—in fact now with increased fervor. His father rose to protect him, asking for mercy and apologizing, asking that the crowd excuse him for his son's madness, the consequence of excessive love.

The pilgrims did not listen. While Qays was bodily carried away from the sanctuary, his blood already washing the road, he repeated in a weak, barely audible voice, "Now You have heard, now You have seen."

Back among his kinsfolk, what he had done and said in the House of God circulated to Layla. She yearned to see him and sent a summons for him. He flew to her despite his disbelief at being invited. Entering her place, he was flushed.

The Citadel's Garden

He is not flesh, but the citadel's garden.

Wounds blossom like roses at the touch of her hand.

This body is for gathering into arms, not for rending. It was made for fingers having mastered the dream and its interpretation.

These eyelashes are meant for evening's repose, to cushion woe's tiny remnants. For you this shoulder to cry upon—may the rivulets intoxicate. Get limbs and elements, add to them this increased issuance of my breath. I will protect you with kohl, with the innermost folds of the heart, with the jewel of the howdahs.

They don't take you from me, or me from you.

She strips him of his shirt, applies two balms: love and poetry. She passes her fingers over his body as if reading it: "All these wounds on such an emaciated body?"

He says, "I await far more. If you will be patient, if you listen to me, if only you are mine, I can endure everything."

What she uttered next
erased from his book
all despair
just as it was nearly crushing
all hope.

You Covered Me, Now Expose Me

Qays ibn al-Mulawwah was asked, "What is the most extraordinary thing that happened to you with Layla?"

He said, "One night guests knocked on our family's door, but we had no provisions. So my father sent me to my uncle al-Mahdi's to ask for help. I stood by his tent, and he said, 'What do you want?' So I told him. He called out, 'Layla, dear, bring out the vat. Fill this boy's container with ghee.' So she brought forth the vessel and started pouring the clarified butter. While close to each other, we began to whisper. Our fingers entwined. Suddenly the ooze poured over my small pot gushing everywhere. I kneeled, sipping the excess from her fingers, moving my mouth up the inner side of her arm. She was pushing me away, but I continued to her shoulders from which her breasts swelled—the unguent liquid leading me to her throat. She was shaking, pushing me away. I inserted my lips where the breasts joined together; her chemise had begun to fall down and away because of the butter racing everywhere. I was tracing its flow finding panthers and tigers bouncing at my face. She said, 'Take my chemise.' So I did, and she said, 'Take me,' so I took her. She said, 'You covered me, now expose me,' so I exposed her—not knowing how the butter made us gush and clot. She said, 'By God, your madness measures well against the reason of the Banu 'Amir, and the first of them is sitting inside this tent'—meaning her father."

Love

Night. Yearning so intense he couldn't sleep. Like a he-wolf following a she-wolf's scent, he began wandering toward her place. Loping ahead, he began chanting her name, over and over, like a paean. As he recited his latest verses to her, his voice shook—he uttered a prayer as if the time for dawn's prayer had come already.

He found her tent, roaming its perimeter, peering into the dark for the special aperture, which she opened for him whenever she was maddened by excitement.

He lifted the slender shred. Her outstretched arms took him in. In a whisper, he begged her to speak to him. Her limbs quaked, casting out her insides split by passion. The supreme sigh escaped her lips. Like a bridge she stretched herself to him, and he listened to the gurgling flask, deep within her, bestowing its water. And he was the vessel into which she poured and he drank.

Every time he would say to her, "More!" She seemed to multiply as the sweat oozed between them. The tent posts swayed, shook as if a hurricane were whirling, clutched at the tattered fabric so that the tent might not fly apart. He had become an overflowing vessel, the sides of their bodies exulting in froth, overcome by sobbing and moaning.

Then she spoke with him about everything, and he listened, obtaining such dazzling pleasure that any lover might feel exalted. The crown that kings brag about became his to wear. She said to him, "What name do you have for this night that stretches out forever?" He said, "Love."

He was the first human to utter the word. He ushered in its meaning. In the language of the Arabs, it came to mean "the description of intimate emotions that dwell beyond description." Never again would the Arabs catch up with such a word of beauty. As for Layla, she fainted when she heard it. She never recovered.

It was said that her name became synonymous with the timeless lovers' night in which desire crackles into exploding madness.

Layl—night—without end.
She became more the metaphor than Qays did.

The Wolf

Distracted in the wilderness, he was asked, "What have you seen in this wild place that's been most beautiful?"

"Layla."

"Yes, yes. But what else?"

"No one but her, I swear."

But then he said, "Only once I did meet a wolf of agile manner and a pleasing odor. I was bent over a young female gazelle stroking her, talking to her—she resembled Layla very much. This wolf waited until I took my hands off her, then the chase was on. I ran, trying to drive him away, but my legs gave out.

They bounded away from me.

"For a time I had to rest. Then I picked up their tracks in the sand. At last I found him. The gazelle had been devoured. I seized an arrow, struck him down. I cut open his belly, extracted the body he had gulped, clutched it to my chest. I stroked it, colored a rag I was carrying with its blood. I drew the rag through my shaggy locks sighing—experiencing an erotic craving like nothing I'd known except with Layla. The pleasure was exquisite to the point that I fainted. When at last I awoke from my swoon, there stood the wolf, as if he had roused himself from a deep nap instead of the death wound I had dealt him. Even more handsome than before, he came with tearful eyes and rubbed his head on my shoulder. I got up, moved alongside him, letting him lead me to the place. From that day on, the wolf never left my side. If I recited verses about Layla, tears would gather in his eyes and a howling more beautiful than the wails of a love-struck human rose from his throat."

The Wedding Night

Majnun wove poetry for Layla that diffused its magic like per-
fume. Everyone knew his verse—the Bedouins who moved from
pasture to pasture, as well as the city dwellers throughout Jazira—
and at last a man called Ward heard of it. He came out of Thaqif of
Ta'if, lured by the tales of Layla, searching for her among the tent
settlements of Banu 'Amir, from the borders of Jazira to its heart-
land. They say Ward memorized the lines of Qays to the point
that when he implored her father for her hand, he kept inserting
the poet's verses into his own prose; that, in fact, he possessed
an intercessor—Qays's verses. It was related that al-Mahdi, the
father of Layla, found in the wealthy Ward of Thaqif a person of
worthy rank, a person holding the power to join or forbid. More-
over, a marriage to Ward would reestablish the limits of tribal
tradition, which Qays and Layla had been flouting. So al-Mahdi,
threatening Layla with the cruelest of punishments, forced her to
take Ward.

On her wedding night, in the center of the tent, she stood up and
addressed Ward: "You have married me because of them and not
because of me. You know my love for Qays and his passion for me;
I warned you about it. But now what's done is done. You know I
possess Qays more in my soul than you will ever possess me in
my body. You accept this now, so you accept it forever. You know
Qays owns the half, the two-thirds, and whatever is left of me.
Your grand office, which gives you the power to join and forbid—
this power with which you came to buy me—holds not the least
sway over me. I announce these things on this night, Ward. If you
hear and accept what I say, then you are my husband in front of
God and man and this is sufficient for you. But Qays is my true
beloved—in front of everyone else—and that is neither sufficient
for him nor me."

It was said: when Ward heard Layla's words, he bowed his head for a long time. Then he looked at her. Standing in front of him, she was a dream trickling between his fingers. He couldn't stanch the flow. Some said Ward saw such a failure was fated, since no one else knew and grasped what lay between Qays and Layla. Still, his ardor for Layla assuaged his loss. So it was that Qays came to inhabit Ward until the man was transmogrified into a shell for the poet-madman. People went on to say that Ward's whole reason to marry was nothing but a doomed desire to possess a dream—the dream that Qays had created in his poetry. And because Ward did not want to squander his fragile, ghostly possession, he had to accept that Layla would never give him more than was her wont.

Crown of Sacrifices

He walks oblivious of things falling—his things—onto the road.

Throat aching. They have told him about the wedding. His skin is on the verge of cracking apart. His hands shrivel, thirsty for water; his innards make music like chants of love-charmed rocks. All the while, howdahs are trailing Layla to the wedding, and the wedding is putting him to death. Covering his inner fires is a tunic of air. He has God. His beloved is prisoner to another man. He walks carrying his corpse. Gazing at dust—the dust of caravans spurring on camels with wedding songs. He is left with remains.

We saw you, O Qays, Crown of Sacrifices.

The Night Described

What emerges—some of it glaringly obvious—from fragments but also from deep readings of the fuller narratives is that Qays did not refrain from Layla after her marriage nor did she abstain from him. When her husband was away, she either received Qays or, if the man were at home, fled to Qays's desolate flatlands or met him on the mountain. It was related by the author of *al-Aghani*, that once, when Layla's husband and her father went to Mecca, she sent a message to Majnun telling him to come right away. He stayed the night, leaving only at dawn, in a state of enchantment. She said to him, "As long as my folk are traveling, come to me." So it was until they came back. It was related that Layla was in such rapture after their final night that she was unable to conceal her intoxication. Freshly home from his travels, Ward was bearing gifts. He was still trying to win her affection: "How do you find this silk fabric and how do you like this perfume, this necklace, and this pendant?" She said, "None of it means anything to me."

Seeing that she kept her distance, he sniffed out what had happened and gathered that Qays had claimed her completely. He folded his gifts away and left.

They say a woman neighbor asked Layla about that night. Layla said, "By God, it was beyond description."

The neighbor said, "How so?" Layla said. "Upon my life, no woman has ever been so completely taken over by a man like him. Never."

Acts of Raving

The record has it that when passion erupted and the ecstatic visions rolled out of him, he would remove all the tent flaps from main rooms and women's quarters alike and cry out to the Banu 'Amir people, "O ye of hard heart, let love penetrate your inner-most and you too will know the splendid shudder. Let your limbs and joints be gratified. Upon your hearts the Angel of Heaven and Hell will flutter its wings. Drop your manual labors, your trading from hand to hand! Let your bodies tangle and ignite. Call every-thing by its rightful name. Say 'it is love' and maybe you will be granted the reality, and its blessings. Then maybe you will savor a little of what possesses me right now. And don't hope for a cure. Don't wish for escape."

Then he went to the tethered horses and camels and undid their ropes while no one was aware. Suddenly they realized that none of their beasts of burden were held down.

That was an act of raving.

Divine Guidance

He did not despair but remained waiting, enchained by her promise of more rendezvous. Layla watched Ward for moments of inattention or distraction, sending word to Qays inviting him to her place. He traveled and came to her as if possessed, while people crossed the road taken by Qays with his things scattered on it. During each moment of waiting, she had been flushing with desire.

He enters her place. She rises to the entrance, tying it closed and letting the curtains down. Qays roves about, enraptured, is on the verge of possessing her like some phantasm guided by magic, goaded by waiting.

They sit clinging to each other, joined by silence more than speech. When he does speak, she pours for him and he says, "Which— you or the drink—will set me on fire and which will put the fire out?" He wonders which part of his body will take in what she next offers and how he can celebrate the grace she bestows. As he talks, she pours herself onto him and no sooner has he sipped a draft than a tumescent sigh erupts from him, honing body and soul. Then the sparks cascade and fires are set ablaze in their garments until they have no escape except to unburden themselves, unwinding the strapping chemises, the cinched coverings over shoulder and the bags lashed to waists. The sheets are yanked apart, cascading here and there. Layla is wallowing in the folds of his remaining garb, he is stealing up her sleeves. She is shoving around with him, he is shaking ecstatically with her in his grip. Her voice quavers, his nocturnal vigil is anointed by frenzy: they ingest the germ of delirium.

The nocturnal wake takes place in a tent with no ceiling until they are touched by day's first prayer call. Then they come out from each other as dreamers come out of a dream.

Worshippers walking to dawn prayers see the madman on their road. "We see you've finally received divine guidance!" they say.

"Oh yes," he says. "I'm now rightly guided."

Each party goes his own way, never again to meet.

The Sun

He was told, "She is but one of many."

He said, "Can there be anyone like her among women?"

He was told, "Many. Many if you want, and they will love you too."

He said, "But I love no one but Layla; among women there exists no substitute."

Annoyed, he moved away from them. "I reveal to them that she is the sun, but they stray from her and become confused. I've almost rolled their noses in her light—perhaps they feel what hell might do to the body. I gesture to them to look at her, but they gaze at my finger and see nothing. They fix on the point of the finger, their pupils dilating until they become night-blind. Their eyeballs start melting, losing sight. In the end perhaps they lose it all."

Water Mirror

She disrobed to bathe. Gazing into the water mirror, she said, "Woe unto him! His attachment to me has devastated him. I am unworthy of such sacrifices and praise. I ask you, by God, is he truthful or lying when he describes me?"

The water-mirror said, "By God, he is truthful. He is not praising but simply describing what his eyes have fallen upon, what his hands have caressed, what all his senses have tasted. He suffers no blame for being crazed by you, and over you."

While she found the answer agreeable, she said, "By the truth of these waters, he deserves from me more than madness. By God, I will give him what he is entitled to, and I will suffer no blame for it."

God Will Forgive

He was told, "Love has led you to this life of suffering."

He said, "And it will end in more than what you see."

Truly his despair was greater than hope; also more beautiful. However, he knew love's path and along it he was making his progress. What he most loved was the playful breeze soughing through his soul.

He was told, "Why don't you pray for God's relief?"

He said, "Were I to ask Him for His forgiveness as often as I think of her, He would forgive my past as well as my future. But no sooner do I pause for prayer than Layla diverts me. God tolerates no partner, just as she tolerates no partner—this I know. But even though polytheism is *haram*, God will forgive me as long as Layla forgives me."

All the Weeping

He was told, "What if Layla were not?"

He said, "I would have wept her into existence."

On Hajj

Various stories have transmitted to us situations that Qays encountered when he was on hajj, suggesting that he travelled to the Holy Sanctuary more than once.

However, our Shaykh Abu Salah Khalaf al-Ghassani—having heard from a villager near the shrine who himself had heard anecdotes about Qays—related:

"He went no more than once, or so we think. And I say 'went,' because he never intended fulfilling hajj. He performed none of our rituals and ceremonial rites. I repeat, this pilgrimage, led by his father who hoped to cure his predilections, was the only one. The trustees of hajj and the custodians of the Holy Kaaba, knowing his awful deed, forbade him entry again into the sanctuary. He acted strangely, reciting poetry—an unprecedented behavior amounting to heresy. This turned people against him, as if he had stirred up the very stones of the Kaaba. If you ask me, Qays came not to publicize his passionate love for Layla and disseminate his amorous poetry—deeds not infrequent during this time. Rather—and God knows best—he came for another purpose. On that day, despite their reticence, many attended to Majnun's poetry, and were touched with a wonder akin to having been charmed. Had it not been for God's almighty power, it would have turned into sedition."

He said, "The villager informed me that when Qays was brought to Mecca, he spent a night talking to himself, like someone raving in his sleep, reproving a woman who was present, though no one saw her. When asked the woman's identity, he swore it was Layla—not as a person but as a she-ass. She was leading an enormous herd of cattle around a turbulent spring that gushed hard upon them, washing but also striking them with force. The cows were driven to circumambulate this spring. They raised a voice to God begging Him to rescind Layla's wrath and to elicit her mercy. But the she-ass did not stop her furious running. Qays asked why she was taking this shape. She said, 'There is in the she-ass something of the scent of prophets.'"

Also it was said that when Majnun's father instructed him to hang on to the Kaaba's sacred drapes in order to forget his love, he obeyed. But no sooner did his hands touch the velvet than he sensed a mysterious life behind them, something spreading between his hands and in front of his eyes, piercing him with sparks of desire. He began wallowing in the drapes as if upon a luxurious couch and cried out so loudly that it shook the entire courtyard of the sanctuary; those on mountaintops heard him:

"O, such enormous clothes! The tiny essence behind this magnificent, spacious chemise is she!" As if in a fever, he began to rhapsodize, sweat flowing over his brow. No one understood how satisfying the moment was for him.

"Another version: 'Ali ibn Muhammad said, 'Then Qays was running between Safa and Marwa, when a call came from above a boulder. Pilgrims stopped running. They hovered around him. I approached and saw a person, whom I learned later to be Majnun; he was calling for a temple to be constructed within the hearts of the people. No sooner did his construction reach to undo the actual stone and mortar temple than I felt my limbs cracking. I was unable to carry myself. My body collapsed from the vehemence of what I heard. My friends carried me to the side, sprinkling water over me to bring me back to consciousness. That was the last I knew of Majnun.'"

Something Other than the Mount

No one knew where Layla was, no news about her doings reached him—he who had grown used to her amorous welcomes. In his eyes, vast spaces narrowed. Her family was working to annihilate him by secreting her away. He began roaming day and night, on the alert for her tent. If he met someone, he said, "What have you heard about Layla, where have they managed to hide her?" Then: "They should have killed me, death would have been easier."

He made for the open spaces. At the same time, her people used the land's vastness to stay away from him. For them, the land expanded. For him, it narrowed. When he inquired about her, the land answered with the shadow of her fugitive steps, with the traces of her perfume sprinkled on her howdah just at the moment of departure. He tore his clothes, fastened his chest to these remnants of her being. He ground his cheeks in the desert's dust and wept out a lament in that newly moist highland. His agitated footprints were drawn across the Jazira sands as he traversed its deserts stretching onward and outward. In his mind, he ascended Mount Tawbad. He decided to set out for the Mount, wandering, lingering between vales and virgin wilderness in the hope that a mirage would arise, then be materialized. Enveloped in loss, he staggered upon the outskirts of Damascus. "Where is Mount Tawbad in the land of Banu 'Amir?" he asked people.

"What do you mean, Banu 'Amir? This is Damascus," they said.

They guided him by the stars. So he wandered beneath the haze of the planets, arriving at the land of Yemen. He'd never seen such country. The people were foreign to him. "Where is Tawbad in the land of Banu 'Amir?" he said to them.

"What land? What Banu 'Amir?"

They steered him again using the stars. Once more he became lost beneath the galaxy. He'd moved beyond what a man can do. Still he went on in his grievous, distracted state until he fell upon the actual Tawbad. He saw something other than the Mount.

Speaking Your Heart

Snippets about her fly in on their own, further confusing his search until he feels he is hearsay's toy. No sooner one account—which he believes—than another greets him. No clear picture forms itself, there is no certainty he can count on. One man told him Layla had been abducted to Iraq. There she became ill, but what could he do, considering where he was? Another voice said she was in Hijaz, then it came about that she was in al-Sifah. Each transmitter embellishes his report according to his inclinations. Qays shouts at them, "You of hardened heart; you conscience-lackers: what you're doing is unacceptable. Someone tell me the truth! In what land dwells my heart? Help me. Stop playing with my soul, it's been devastated by suffering. You point me toward every direction, inciting me to take up nothing but wandering, making certain I find only mirages. Isn't there one among you who possesses the truth? Are you out to make a Majnun crazy? Woe unto you!"

Passion roiled. Home, neighborhood, desert—they narrowed in on him. The deserted places that he'd been raised on became a refuge large enough to encompass his love, offering him noble friends. He found in wolves, mountain goats, birds, and trees the kindred natures in which his soul could be calm and his body relaxed. His shade followed the sun, his eyes fascinated by the power that grants grass its color. He never asked the spring's water where it came from or who it was, knowing water washes the heart's affairs, erases from shoulders the dust of the road. Such a desolate region furnished his room with quietude, safeguarding his dreams a place to sleep. He who dwells in the wilderness owns it. Those who glimpsed him saw a herd of wolves trotting in front and behind, guarding his every step; for love implies that you can only be moved by passion. The desolate place: a citadel that envelops and protects.

He was dragging his limbs across the bulges at the foot of Mount Tawbad, in a tattered condition, eating nothing but the grass shoots among the rocks and taking his drinks with mountain goats. He met a wolf that sat next to him. The wolf sought to guide him, to pacify his soul, to allow the humors a chance to recover their balance. He began following the wolf as if he were charmed. Together they set out for the Place. When they got to it, they entered so that Layla could come to them. The Place was a clean reception hall. You step on its floor and you hear the thrumming of feet. Beside it are velvet-like carpets of delightful herbs, telling you this is yours—and you feel it is yours. A light wind clasps you. You take my hand to guide you but you find your own way and your eyes are not bedazzled by the horizon of the reception hall. A languid blueness calls you, you go.

Qays sobs: "I saw her! Layla was in a howdah and I sat next to her. Tell me she is here, then go."

The wolf said, "Stay and speak your heart. She will hear you and come. You will never be alone."

The wolf leaves and Layla appears as both water and angel. It seems that he is seeing it all.

The Text and the Account

I am coming—coming to you—you who are not in doubt and I who am not unaware. The road and its icy hardships, this silence and its single inferno, have tormented me. I have suffered from too much wilderness, too much desert. Your expectations of me are unfulfilled. Your messages to me remain unanswered. For I am coming: there is no escape, no salvation from what we chose, except to recall that we did choose it. I am coming so grant me time without limit, be excessive with your affection, afflict us both with pleasure; as for others, let them choose their own afflictions. Let me have all the downy feathers of your shoulder. I will lay my head there and weep out all the weeping until my liver combusts, shooting out flames, fervors, vapors of longing. Attend to all the forged, erroneous accounts—attend but don't believe. Defeated knights with their armies of assertions lay heaped upon your shoulder claiming their absurd victory. But you: mind your delicate shoulder and its downy softness. Listen for the howling of the wolf, be sensitive to the lament of the heavy heart. You owe me a debt, which I shall pay instead of you; and I owe you a debt, which you will pay to me. Both of us are now in an enchanted world. What we've become, we can't escape. Believe that I am coming one night with shuddering heart, eyes aching, crazed within my breastbone, my bared body searching for your bosom, storing its paradise for me. Come! Part the chemise yielding me total entrance when I come and total release when I must go. Re-pledge yourself to the night vigils; don't doze or miss the dream. In the hour when I descend on you like an archangel bearing annunciation, believe that I worship only you, never given to doubt; he who emanated from you, he who sings paeans to no one but you, possessing no goal but you. Make your tent a cosmic reception hall, a galaxy pavilion. Turn your bed into a nebula. Tie the tent flap open. Let all dwellers—of desert and city alike—enter and witness the fighting and contending of our bodily parts. They rub against each other, flare up, smacking together—light flying, flames gushing out. Leave the tent unguarded, as if you were no longer there, so they can descend upon us and gulp at what we do. This way they will no more doubt the text and the account.

Heart Madness

"If I swore Majnun of Banu 'Amir was not mad, I would be telling the truth."

So saith Ibn Salam and we believe him. Not because he swore, but because intimacy forms its own argument. Something in the heart points us that way. It is a blessing that someone disputes his madness. His verse does not contain the thread of madness—not if that term means folly, insanity, or abnormal mental fragility. Manifestations of extreme craving and mounting fascination for the Other bordered his life like two ends of a parenthesis. From the days of yore, poets have owned such a nature, here multiplied by the passion of love. Look to his verse for the indications, the interpretations. We write what appeals to our spirit, what stirs our imagination with its strangeness, what corresponds and makes sense in linking the text with the account. When a statement emanates from the sense of heart—craziness—we accept it, take it up, add to it and hyperbolize it. So when a like statement is taken to reduce Qays to pathology, we dismiss it and pay it no further heed. The tale we have brought together appeals to two types of people: poets and lovers—and in all of us, there is a measure of both.

Madness as Mask

"A little confused, yes. But not mad."

Al-Asma'i, O God, wants us to keep confusion apart from frenzy. Do words overflow with meanings beyond those that the carafes of dictionaries pour out? Does legacy mean anything other than the inheritance of first sayings? Aren't texts—body and notes—controlled by their exegeses? Should we say that we are mad while they are confused? Are we the cups and they the carafes? Which of us is the wine and which, the intoxication?

He found madness to be a convenient cover for that which others could not comprehend. This cover allowed him to pursue his desires beyond the pale of accepted reason. He was dedicated to Layla's comprehending this chosen posture, and she did intuit that his madness was like a mask that allowed them the privacy in which to utter secret messages and recite verses together. Madness became that mysterious coda that branded the being of Qays and granted Layla her peculiar essence. "Verily, my mad passion for Layla has triggered her madness."

She whispered to Qays alone, "The love I have for you is more than the love you have for me."

Should we consider her pronouncement a form of madness because it is passion-driven? Or is her love so passionate because it is, in fact, madness? Our long-standing knowledge is that a madman does not say such things about himself, unless he, by negating negation, ends up affirming.

The Royal Road

If being mad would spare him their evil, then let him be mad. Far stronger than this ruse, however, was their violence. Separating then concealing Layla from him, they forced her into an impoverished union. He, detained and oppressed, became an animal to chase, disowned, expulsed by edict from the tribe. Madness became the only reasonable refuge from what they condemned. Most probably Qays contributed to the dissemination of his madness in more than one place. His verses, which alluded to madness as God's will—quoting al-Kalbi's vindication of insanity—were often used by those who wanted to categorize him as mad. Al-Asfahani transmitted an incomplete account, which we have supplemented:

"A man from Najd heading to Damascus was caught by nocturnal rain in the desert. He saw a tent, made for it, and was welcomed by the guardians of a caravan. Among them was a middle-aged woman whose comeliness had not been compromised, as if she were holding onto a beauty that refused time's victory. She said, 'What do you know of the Banu 'Amir of Najd? Do you know of their kinsman called Qays, known as Majnun?' He responded, 'I was walking with a person who had been his companion when young. He caused me to stop near Mount Tawbad and told me—based on his father's account—that Qays used to frequent this place, finding comfort in its desolateness. This man, Qays, would not divulge his feelings nor leave his besotted dreams of infatuation unless Layla were mentioned.'

"The woman wept so much that I worried about her. 'Why are you crying?' I said. She said, 'I am Layla of whom Qays sang, teaching the Arabs to love.' I said, 'And what of his madness?' She said, 'It was nothing of the sort, just my way of resisting the tribe and his way of feigning distance from its authority. Madness was the silken weave of our royal road to paradise. What could folk do with two people dwelling outside all assigned meanings, enveloped like sword and sheathe—outside the measures of right and wrong? Their propriety locks away any intimacy of the soul, while our kind of madness sets free the fated heart. The honey of joy rises like an essence from the text, like some rose of ecstatic flesh. What does it matter if one is called mad when the spirit has been untethered? I was crazier about him than he of me, but little do they reason such things. He is, by God, the most rational, most brilliant man that a human female on earth or a she-djinn beneath the earth has ever embraced. For he who declaims such poetry is, by God, mad-hearted—but they took it further than that. We reveled and relished our rendezvous while they painted him askew.'

"I asked her, 'Are you still in love?' She said, 'As ever. Never have I come across a man who can love like him, can warm my flesh with poetry as he did.' I said, 'What about your desire for him now?' She said, 'Desire lives on, though the instrument be damaged.'"

A Two-Way Lantern

And it came to be that they were deluded. They couldn't detect the gulf between madness of mind and the madness of heart that contains all poetry, all love.

A mind that overcomes gold took wing, bearing an annunciation of its heart-madness to those sick with love in the air of al-Jazira, but jolting those whose insides were toughened against love, while awakening the somnolent-hearted, tempting maidens to part their chemises to youths almost as ruined by love as they— these young men, fondly, relentlessly pushed their shoulders toward the most obvious of perils; getting women to denounce their husbands, siding instead with the shari'a of love.

Thus people discovered joy. Undulant sighs rose behind every screen to fill the night. A whole people, possessed; every lover snipping off strips of his woman's garments from every side and every woman raising the first toast to her deep cavern, swaying the lantern of crystallites that guides the lover while confusing all others. There was no madness. There was a woman named Layla, of whom it was said she was all women. And it was said she was queen of djinns who revealed herself to one person, gave herself to one man, so he took her. Then he passed his spirit into every passerby, every resident, every coward who ever concealed his love for a woman, exposing every woman hiding her infatuation for someone other than her husband.

His name became synonymous with infamy: Qays. All around the land the shedding of his blood became lawful. Swords sought him out. But no sooner did these weapons find him than their holders appealed to him, "Don't stop."

And he did not stop.

Enticement

Al-Asfahani—the most prolific transmitter of Majnun's accounts

with brilliant command in weaving and unweaving Majnun's

chronicles—related in his *Aghani* all that compromises a

complete report, a firm account, a coherent text, or a

definitive position. No doubt this was a sign that

al-Asfahani's narrative failed to verify the full

account, opting for the pleasing text. Thus

the truth of such assertions contains no

significance. Transmitters monkey

with the truths of lives, their

anecdotes making

monkeys of us,

while poetry

entices.

Towards It at Every Turn

Inmates of an asylum report: Qays spent time with them. He was the sharpest in intelligence, the most competent debater, even among seasoned physicians. He divulged a secret, swore the inmates not to disclose it while he lived. He had found the mask of madness to be the safest, most elegant garb for winning Layla. All subsequent tales of this madness had sprung from an initial ruse to camouflage the satirical verses he composed, as a youth, about al-Mahdi, Layla's father. "When al-Mahdi complained about me to Caliph Marwan ibn al-Hakam, a certain man of letters named Asma'i fashioned the story of my madness, thereby preserving me from the sultan's wrath. But al-Mahdi did not forgive me. When al-Asma'i was asked later about me, he denied my madness in a locution that suggested, in fact, a total affirmation of my madness. Thus he succeeded in disseminating this rumor, which lives on to our day. I suspect the majority of chronicle transmitters coming after him did not accept the claim of my madness, dismissing all accounts and considering only my poetry as evidence. In madness, they detected a disposition concealing more than it reveals. For them, the more ambiguous an account, the more its dissemination multiplies and the more its audience is held in thrall. I am sure that al-Asfahani himself was quite certain in *al-Aghani* that the claim of madness was false. But he was oblique about it so that subsequent readers would not sneeze at his compositions."

The transmitters did not bother to verify this record of the asylum inmates until a shaykh of indefinite time and unknown place, a man called 'Abd al-Rahman Sahib al-Muluk, came along and documented the issue. Tayyib al-'Ud related to us, on the authority of Dhabih al-Jund, "Sahib al-Muluk addressed me, saying, 'The chronicle transmitters unconsciously used to negate what they wove of Qays's accounts of madness with verse of his that they transmitted. His is a poetry that cannot be composed by a deficient mind. In fact, it points to a serene disposition, to an alert intellect, and to a refined sensibility. It reveals an imagination of sublime beauty and originality. There is no muddling or yammering—the likes of which characterize the mentally deficient—anywhere in his text. For this reason, the madness attributed to Qays was probably the outcome of the troubled link between inconsistent accounts of Qays that repel readers who, on the other hand, find themselves entranced by the poetry's well-calculated, proper images that pique and captivate the imagination. Any attending tales of madness will sound amiss, thereby crumbling into nothing when we encounter the contradiction that surfaces in the statements about the dictated lawful shedding of Qays's blood on the one hand and his madness on the other. For it is commonly known that the lawful shedding of blood applies only to men of sound mind who have gone outside customary law. I mean criminals, highway robbers—fugitives wanted by law, tracked down by those who seek justice in blood revenge or who hunt such men for reward. So how could Qays's blood be lawfully shed when he suffered a mental affliction that disqualified him from awareness of his actions, hence responsibility as well? I believe the Qays legend that transmitters wanted to convey through their Arabic narratives slipped out of their hands and took directions no one could dream of. So Qays—thanks to his madness—became free not only from the power of the sultan and the tribe, but also—and especially—from the boundaries imposed on him by the transmitters of his story. We still find him stepping out and escaping, over and over.'

If Qays is unpredictable in his behavior, if he is untamed and appears as a wild man, this is the very nature of poets and lovers. Such behavior is accepted since these two follow the dictates of their imagination, roving, taking all paths to enticement."

Love: So Many Doors

So many doors. The lot crossed by Qays. The rest of us, lingering at thresholds.

The door of affection: Your preferred garment when getting ready to feast. The fur of the air kissing, wounding you. You wend your way to intimacy. Childhood's in the vicinity. Its shadows flicker at the edge of your eye, you glance its way. Become tame.

The door of longing: Nocturnal waves gather round you like a strange boat. A good swimmer, you drown. No distractions now. Yours alone. The smoldering rose blooms as the wind picks up strength.

The door of craving: Sighs of heaven. Souls entering the realm of magic. Nothing else exists but It. Tattered slumber, a half-existing dream. You fly in the feathers and wings, no way to truly rest.

The door of infatuation: It torments you, makes you calm as indigo; you become transparent. A delicate mind, a lofty madness. You alone are for It. You recall, you forget; you don't return. You luxuriate in delights of the senses.

The door of desire: Wedding of humors. The Terror of elements. Heaven and Hell and everything between. The two of you, alone. You tremble in absence and presence. A malady without cure. All of it, yet not enough.

Herself Eroticized

It was related, on the authority of Abu Anmar Ibrahim Ibn ʿAbdallah, that he came upon verses of Qays, which he considered candid, unrestrained descriptions of his love affair's core. Even Abu Anmar—known for his fine taste in reading poetry of glowing desire, examining it with the throbs of his own heart—considered these lines of Qays some of the most powerful love poems of his time:

"Let it be known, if the husband of Layla is among you:
By His Throne, eight times I have kissed her dew
I swear by Him, the Almighty, I have seen her
When twenty fingers, hers, were on my back askew."

Abu Anmar, uncharacteristically belabored, saying, "We have only to imagine the twenty fingers of Layla, entangled on Qays's back as she is clinging to him, his forefront in her lap, to grasp that they did not pass their time weeping and lamenting whenever a chance meeting was offered, as successive stories try to claim."

Some condemned this interpretation and considered such unlawful acts farfetched and alien to what Majnun's poetry exudes. When they were asked, "Honorable Masters, what is intended by unlawful?" arguing along Ibn Jawziyya's position in his work on Women that "some claim that the lover is entitled to the upper half of his beloved's body, from her navel upwards, and can obtain from it what he wishes—hugging, kissing, and sucking—while the other half is for the husband."

Such were the conventions of pre-Islamic Arabs. It was related that Layla's female neighbors entreated her to tell them about her relationship with Qays and whether he confined himself to the upper half. She retorted, "Haven't you called him the Madman?

You don't know one tenth of what I experience unless there be madmen like him around."

They asked for more details, so she added, "At that moment, halters and bridles slip away, and the steering is neither limited to one nor can the two together handle it. Boundaries become senseless as mist descends erasing all signs and contours, coming neither to the aid of sight nor to the aid of insight. Un-numbered senses begin to engage such that we hardly know if we are in a dream or we, ourselves, are pure dream. Those who utilized an astrolabe to tell the time and pattern for love failed to articulate for us which of the two halves is lawful—*halal*—for the woman-beloved in the body of the man-lover. At that moment we know not who kindles the body of the other and who quenches, who is the ember and who is the air."

Kalam ibn Wahsh

So it was said: Qays frequented a jurist, a *faqih*, named Kalam ibn Wahsh seeking juridical counsel, *fatwa*—concerning people's ever-multiplying indictments—if indeed his relations with Layla amounted to fornication.

Kalam said, "Fornication is the granting of your body to someone you don't love. But when love and true yearning are present, then proceed with union. It is not fornication. Not in God's decree."

The account goes on. Kalam leaned over Qays whispering, "O my son, be in love as much as you can, enjoy what is feasible by Islamic law and, as long as possible, don't turn off the firebrand of love by marrying."

That Majnun followed Kalam's edict is further recorded.

Laughter

Shaykh 'Abd al-Qadir ibn Salih ibn 'Aqil—ardent chronicler of love-madness—said, 'Abd al-Hamid, the leading biographer—though unreliable as such—told me on the authority of our own Shaykh Abu Salah Khalaf al-Ghassani who, in turn, received word from Abu Anmar Ibrahim ibn 'Abdallah, asylum inmate, himself repeating the words of a man who did not reveal his name and it was of no import to us:

"Once I happened upon the tents of Qays and the palm trees of Layla's family. A summer's night. Suddenly laughter from afar. I hurried along, the laughter becoming clearer though blended with a sobbing that brought me up cold, if but for a moment. Drawing closer, I detected derision in the laughter. It was Qays ibn al-Mulawwah from Banu 'Amir tribe. He was alone, sitting on the earthen floor giggling continuously. No sooner did a burst of laughter end than he was sobbing, exhaling, kicking with arms and legs in the sand. On mastering his breath again, yet another burst of laughter seized him. I could not believe my eyes. It didn't make sense: Qays never smiled. I drew closer, studied him. The man was in another world. Occasionally he wound down, seeming to reflect on something. But not for long. Another attack of impudent, resounding laughter would yank him out of his surroundings.

"At first I thought, 'Here is Majnun of Banu 'Amir gone mad.' Then I thought, 'But how can the man go mad when he's mad already?' I stayed put long enough to make sure I wasn't assailed by confused dreams or by the muddling delusions of the solitary desert. But this Qays was no convenient phantom. 'Listen, man,' I said, 'are you Qays ibn al-Mulawwah, associated with Layla of Banu 'Amir?'

"Bubbling and gurgling, he was swept over by laughter again. He swayed, tossed himself on the sand, toiled to control himself, then turned to me and said, with no interest, 'I may be he, but God knows best.'

"Then a fresh attack tore him away from himself. He rose to his feet, moving away while the laughter radiated like a struck gong into the night. Impervious to my question as to what provoked such laughter, he left me bewildered, a state typical of one who cannot believe his eyes. I got hold of my limbs, ran to the tents shouting, 'Get up! See what wonders have befallen Qays; the man who doesn't smile is laughing.'

"No one believed me. They gathered round in a state of agitation. Just as I was swearing by all things sacred, the echoes of his resounding laughter reached us. Lo, the figure of a man materialized. It was Qays ibn al-Mulawwah himself. Everyone began asking about the condition in which he was roving. 'By God Almighty,' he said, 'I don't know why I haven't done this since I first fell in love with Layla, because what's happening now is exactly what happened when I first became infatuated with her. God—O God!—perpetuate in me this condition until the Day of Judgment.'

"He walked away without the matter getting any clearer."

Transmitters differ in their interpretations of this incident. One said he sat with Majnun in one of his half-present moments and listened while he went over the event:

"'I was spending the night with Layla in her tent. When our time was done, I left in the direction of my people on the other side of the valley. As soon as I entered my tent, I saw, to my amazement, Layla sitting on my mat. I came out like a madman, walked straight back to Layla's tent. Storming into it—I had to know immediately whether I could trust my eyes—I was struck down again. There she was, fixing herself after our rendezvous. With no further delay I turned and retraced my steps. There again I saw Layla. I went back to Layla's tent, found her there; then again to my tent to find her in that place also. I came and went more than nine times. She was in both places at once. I wavered between believing what I saw and denying what I wished. I was bewildered, almost senseless. How to account for such a thing? I was plunged into a state of mind I'd never encountered before: guffaws rang from my mouth like a spring whose seal has been ripped off, and the next thing I knew someone was saying, Why such loud laughter?

"'Transmitters of my story, in all their compendious accounts, fail to mention this incident. I can no longer conceal from you that, after my love for Layla, the most beautiful thing for me was this laughing attack.'"

The chroniclers, apparently, disavowed the laughing account. They based their logic on the fact that Qays's essential portrait is the same in all chronicles; it does not change, should not change. No, they said, a passionate love like Qays's does not admit smiling. Laughing, giggling, jeering? Impossible.

An interpolation in the biography of Majnun, they called it: sullying the grave and melancholy image associated with his name.

There was a consensus among chroniclers of authority and those lesser chroniclers who imitate them: the account of Qays' laughing spells is considered frivolous, needlessly confounding. If Abu Anmar claimed such an incident really happened, then his stay in a mental asylum says the rest.

However, we—your poet and his ilk—have found in this variant something we can trust without confirming, despite the probability that it may well approach lying. We hold this position because of an auspicious fragment by Qays:

"As some lovers falsify . . ."

As poets, like Qays, we must say there is more to a created corpus than factual history.

The Argument

It's said that people told Qays, "Wake up, for lovers have woken
    up"
But he did not do so.
". . . and he who once owned flames of the heart watched them
    die out"
        But he did not do so
". . . and he who suffered the anxiety of lovers has calmed down"
        But he did not do so
". . . and he who preoccupied himself with women now knows
    boredom"
        But he did not do so
". . . and those who went too far in their cravings came back"
        But he did not do so
". . . and those enslaved by love forgot"
        But he did not do so
". . . and those excessively lured gave up"
        But he did not do so
". . . and those at fault repented"
        But he did not do so.

Good for him. If he'd done any of these things we'd have no argu-
ment against those contending we love too much.

The Discerning Lantern

A Banu 'Amir tribesman was asked, "Do you know the madman among you murdered by love?"

He responded, "What you say couldn't be true. Love kills the weak-hearted only. If Qays were killed, the agent would not be love. Look for a person."

This disavowal is a lantern guiding us to what our hearts know already. The obvious injustice that befell Qays led to his premeditated murder. Qays was watched in every vale by many enemies who might well have spared him that long wait for a natural death. The author of *al-Aghani* related that Qays had two paternal half-brothers. Among them, he was the one famed for love, poetry, and good conduct. The youngest, he was also the highest-minded, the loftiest in esteem. He enjoyed solitude. After he'd been denied the pleasure of human company, he embraced the wilderness. He befriended the beasts.

"By God," his father was recorded as saying, "he was my favorite. He of all the young men was the most handsome, the most youthful, the most eloquent, the most charming, and the best declaimer of poetry. When the young men conversed, his articulation rose above the others. I was proud of him. And still am."

Being the preferred son made his brothers jealous. After his poems and love became famous, their jealousy turned to spite. They conspired with his enemies and incited the authorities against him. As for Layla's rigid folk, they did not find in Qays a man of sufficient rank—they who have the august right of gathering and disbanding people. Social rank had never drawn Qays nor concerned him. In childhood he persisted in playing with Layla, in youth he became enamored of her, and when the flames of love began to move in her blood, he flirted with her. This condition tore at their very being, while maligning their reputation in the desert. It is said that when love overpowered Qays and when al-Mahdi's rejection agonized him, he journeyed among the tribes. He announced his love for Layla and tried to mobilize people against the wrongs of those who don't esteem love, those who value it less than commerce.

So al-Mahdi and his toadies raised a hue and a cry with religious authorities saying his faith was in question.

Never or He Dies

According to *al-Aghani*, Qays "abandoned prayer. When asked, 'why do you not pray,' he said nothing. We fettered him, but he bit his tongue and lips so terribly we freed him to wander."

People railed that his poetry dishonored religion, thus they dubbed him "sinner":

"You—who are enraged by God's will, objecting to His verdicts."

They cited his deeds at the Kaaba when he invoked profane love instead of reverence. They said he attended to the soothing east wind instead of meditating upon the Prophet's grave, where he stood. *Al-Aghani*'s author, adding to what we're seeking now, said the kinsfolk of Layla announced that Majnun might never again enter their domiciles without dying—the sultan having legalized the shedding of his blood.

This threat, alongside rumors vended by slanderers, melded with various wishes in the tribe to ruin Qays. At times their pretext was his violation of the tribe's customs and at others his irreverence for religion, but mostly it centered on his relationship with Layla.

So they came together from all sides. On the one hand, they confined Layla to her husband, while on the other hand they tightened the grip of isolation in the wilderness on Qays. He prolonged his stay there, escaping the sultan's terror and keeping secret the few nights when Layla stole to him, unbeknownst to others.

It is said that for a period there was no news of him. Then in a valley where there is no sown land, someone stumbled upon his corpse, surrounded by stones, head cracked, brains scattered about, limbs beaten and throat cut, the blood still forming a rivulet where a she-gazelle stood, drinking of its crimson, shading his body from midday's solar immensity.

The maidens in the vales and from the towns poured forth—forgetting their veils—screaming and lamenting. Young men huddled together weeping and sobbing. The kinsfolk of Layla came forward to offer their condolences; with them the uneasy al-Mahdi was saying, "He killed himself" and "I did not have a hand in his misfortune. God, grant no forgiveness to he who pushed us all to such an ending."

It is said no day ever witnessed more women weeping or more men sobbing as the day when Qays died.

It Is Love

Proclaim: It is Love,
compelling air and glass,
exposing the soul's psalmody,
the doves' recitation.
Proclaim it: It is Love
and listen not but to the heart,
flee from indifference,
cast off afflictions of anxiety
invoked by the water of words.
Tell them now: Between
God's Book and Desire
your exhortations flow
and the mist of creation rains
upon the fire of the tents.
Proclaim while they slumber
in dreams:
you will see in the desert narcissus,
in the lute's melody,
in the mist of poetry,
narration and wreckage.
Proclaim it: It is Love
and what collapses, collapses,
there being naught beyond perfumed spice
except the unknown of deserts,
the details of escape,
naught but the sand-crown
deposed at our feet.
The eye of the dust reads
what is left for us
and what has no end,
let it not end

like death's secret—
what remains for us
being mere suicide.
Proclaim it: It is Love,
an angelic road for which we cry
and on which we cry,
if only we had a tent
in the earthly paradise.
If only we have God's apple
we would kneel between His hands.
Whenever he divulges a secret to us,
we become intimate
and glorify Love for Him
and take a night journey to Him.

Proclaim it: It is Love
as if God did not sympathize
with other than you,
did not listen except to you,
as if there were no madman in the world
but you,
as if God existed to erase people's
sorrow in your heart,
to redeem you with what will place
your secrets in the angel's crown.
Proclaim it: Love
led Layla to a night journey,
guided Qays to the waters of ruin.
Proclaim it: It is Love that sees you.

Selected Poems

Al-'Amal al-Shi'riyya [Poetic Works]. 2 vols. Beirut: Al-Mu'sasa al-'Arabi-
yya lil-Dirasat wal-Nashr, 2000.

Da' al-Malak [Leave the Angel Alone]. Damascus: Dar Kan'an, 2009.

In the Sun's Eye

Vol. 1: 40–41

Child of the sun's eye
raise your bronze forearm
and take tomorrow's dawn
raise your rose-crowned head
and strike the strings of the lyric
in this world no strings fear the human
          touch so strongly.

Child of new day
day born in yesterday's wound
wield your father's hammer
crack the barriers of history-corrupt.
Are you wounded in the street?
So long as your pens are strong
refusing to walk a road
          backward,
so long as your iron is hot,
then hammer away,
maul your chains into a knife
and plant it—O child—

          into the eye
          that fears your sun.

Tell Us, O Scheherazade

Vol. 1: 66–69

Tears stream down night's cheeks,
Scheherazade folds her torn black *'abaya*,
begins narrating in the eye of internal day
tales of truth,
imagination having killed itself:

Oceans filled the eyes
of sad Penelope—
watering, sailing tears.
For a thousand years
her miserable spindle extolled in darkness,
through crucified nights, prostrated in awe.
For a thousand years
her Arabian knight had been yearning for mainland,
gazing at the moon that begat time,
stretching his arm familiar with fights,
ever stretching, tightening the sail
that makes the spindle's thread grow longer.

O distant sanctuary,
absence grows long,
youth-wasting Penelope chants
an unceasing song of spindles and suffering,
she too increasing the thread of life—
O distant sanctuary.

Behind the walls of darkness
wolves howl: we crave you, O moon goddess,
we aim to chase down our desires.
The Arabian knight overruns all hurdles,
every day a life ending,

the rain agonizing
over every piece of ground washed
by sand and wind thrust like a knife
into rock's heart.
From their depths, from their seashells and giant pearls,
oceans shove him yet farther away,
this knight in exile. On the shore, Penelope
waits for news, yearning to hear
the sea chant,
the fulsome *hulu* cast from horseback,
the heart-tune of her adventurous knight,
crossing the lowlands in triumph.

Such were the nights
when Penelope spun illusions
that gulled the nights,
extending bridges for reunion,
conjuring her knight feared by men to come forth.

Absence grows long,
longer and longer.
When will he return, return? My hands ache,
my eyes grow dim beholding the spindle,
my thread is wasting away to nothing.
Still, no return.
O knight, shall I spray the road with my blood,
spin from my hair a *thawb*
and devour the fire?
O knight, when will you return?

So sad Penelope feeds night to day,
a heart task—passion, yearning, fervor.
She goes on narrating the tale of the Arabian
to the wounded night.

Tears drench her grieving-shawl.
Meanwhile he is stranded on sea peaks,
surviving on sahara sand,
bones for a chest.
On the road a fire still flickers;
another day gone, Penelope.
Your knight has not come to day's moon.
Instead he explores saharas,
the oceans, the waiting . . .
he goes on, exploring.

Evening arrives. Scheherazade folds
her darkly black *'abaya*.

O Scheherazade, tell us.
O Scheherazade.

Alphabet of the Arab Twentieth Century: *Alif*

Vol. 1: 117–18

The issue differs,
the alphabet we live in is new
we write not on water
but draw blood stanzas.
The intrepid poet admits.
He dips his quill in wounds,
wrestles with wind,
suffers the long journey.
The new poet in our new time differs,
the question, O comrade, differs,
the issue differs.

You Are the Music, I Am the Dance

Vol. 1: 242

Forbidden dance
     in the sweeping vales
        I
undulate
           You
     my music

Plants swell
     alongside me
     a storm arises
the nipple of youth
     sighs
     all in my step

walking   not on earth
flying   not in air
     I
the dance
     You
        the music.

All of Them

Vol. 1: 244

They all said there's no use
they said   I'm leaning on the sun's dust
my beloved
            before whose tree
        I stand   is unapproachable
they said   I am mad
    for placing myself
in the volcano's lap   singing
they said   that salty mountain never
dispenses a jot   of wine
they said it's impossible
to dance   on one leg
she will not succumb to such invitations
they said   your night party takes place   with no lights
they said
they said
all of them said
                        then arrived at the party
on time
the lot of them

I Don't Bow Down

Vol. 1: 245

Standing in the wind's ice, naked
alone like the letter *alif*
I do not bow down
I revolt against all gods
and do not bow down
I escape fire, enter its double
but do not bow down
the intersection of contradictions
I believe in it
and do not bow down
I mix myself up with ashes
but do not bow down

except to you.

With More Freedom

Vol. 1: 258–59

Freely   I set up relations
with words
in the inkpot
of your delectable inferno
I dip my quills
and write
        you were first to read
my bleeding

From your lap I was yanked
they proscribed my pens, papers
they parted me from books
from your warmth (which made my words
        glimmer)
my fingers
        on their own—in the cell's darkness—
sought out luminous roads
leading to the Word
I stopped needing pens, papers,
I read and embraced my comrades' hearts
I established relations with the horizon

when I am at sea or in the sahara
in stony jungle
        or in the special state
poetry cannot depart
the poet needs but true yearning
and the gushing begins

Nor can you be taken away
your yearning stirs   like a light
within these words

Adventure

Vol. 1: 293

Let me steal beneath your robes
      just once
I will not scratch your ivory
heaped up like treasure
I know you—
            diaphanous like a butterfly's wing—
so let me enter once
where the warmth of coffee
makes the nocturnal soiree
sweeter yet
just once
I will be the polite child
watchful of decorum's limits
here is how it will be
I will enter from the lip of the collar
but how will I get out?
      I would not want to.

The Intimate Inferno

Vol. 1: 299–300

Winter   desert   solitude
cactus . . .
night   silence

Everyone descending the deep wells of sleep . . .

                 equipped with dreams
I wander night's forests
limbs exhausted
shrieking like a lost plucked seagull
longing so much for rest

Letters   words   splinters
phantasms   flashes on the pillow
comrades on the move from unfinished dreams
          entering a dream yet to begin

still I can't subside

like a crazy swinging wave . . .
     on the foot of a foolish giant
still I can't subside
Paradiso mingling with Inferno in my fervent scream
still I can't subside

in the morning   the comrades stir
they find in my bed the sick body
     and the poem
        that breeds life

Illumination

Vol. 1: 422

In the captured calm
of the cameleer's song
while tribes venture
onto verdant days
I, spent in proud despair,
squat in my captivity
forgetting, remembering,
    forgetting

Earth's Mantle

Vol. 1: 429

Who will collect the tears and confer them to the mother
her son's absence tries her
she goes into the street veil-less
casts about for tears sufficient to cover the earth
let her have her tears
let her have relief so she can bear
     her son's wandering.

History

Vol. 1: 435

Those who were:
were once.

Love Feast

Vol. 1: 470

My table is open to passersby
to vagabonds, blacks, rejectionists, dervishes, thieves
Sufis, Carmathians, pirates
and those who question   who doubt
and those whose swords know no cases but chests
swords   that came from God
                    to God returning.

The Dream Chapter

Vol. 1: 475

O fourth impossible
     take pity on me
         become

Genesis

Vol. 1: 480

Quivering, this earth.
        Where can I put down my foot?

A Dynasty

Vol. 1: 498–99

His mother said,
you descended from a man who mixed the sea with iron
carried you toys from the sea
where the sea star becomes a seahorse
and from blood comes ink and writing
he who gazed at the sand
lost in thought, captivated,
conferred on you rings, seals, and helmets
he did not get tired
the iron got tired of him as did the waves, the elements.
You descended from all that. Where will you go now?

I shall wander, O mother
I dream of becoming a poet
mixing the elements, quaking them
juxtaposing them   harmonizing
building crowded bridges
          no room for anyone on them.

O mother,
          when will I become a poet   when will
I have children and a wife who tells them:
you descended from a man who mixes nipples

with night visions

The Charmed

Vol. 1: 501

He lights the house's lone candle,
opens the door to the nocturnal room,
his gift from the ancestors.
His first foot pressing forward,
he penetrates the lampless space,
veers with his witness-candle,
seeking out the dark.
The candle expires, he lights it,
expires again, he lights it.
Matchsticks low, he cannot find the dark.

Memory of All That

Vol. 1: 528

They can forbid coffee, apertures, and notebooks
they can fence the trees, the river, the legends
they can pack the forests
                in jars and belts
they can block the roads
                of both mail and bees.
These graceful shores
they can turn into graveyards, parking lots for spiders
their clutches roam freely among the wind,
the mausoleum, and the parade.
They can do all that
but not forgetting
they have done all that
is ours to choose.

The Stars' Messenger

Vol. 1: 540–41

The banners crowded the horizon
    leaning, plunging forward
purple seeping from them
their verdure embracing the sand
the camel litters shaking, seductive
    a treasure house crowded with gifts
I saw the banners when lightning was their roof
rippling as at the wedding parade
it might have been the wine
the shy maidens covering their breasts
with young men's chests and shouting
the earth was frenzied
the banners washed by clouds
    at heaven's gate
banners in the insomnia of creation
What? I asked
    a martyr marrying the earth,
    this—his commemoration.

The Captain

Vol. 2: 44

He built his ship, straightened its towers, banners gulping the
    breeze.
He belted the water with lighthouses,
sea gulls alone knowing the light, the time, the turning of
    constellations.
He filled the ship's galley with wine and bread,
loosed the gangplanks for willing sailors,
prepared his sails: whiteness vast as a cosmos filling the horizon
and there he stood   the loftiest mast
guarding, waiting for his men.

It was late. Very late   he remained standing.

The Waters of Meaning

Vol. 2: 78

I fraternized with chaos, my hands surrendering to its seduction.
I turned my body into a language-vessel, sketching with
    ambiguity a fissure
in the earth: its narratives, an image mixing water with words.
I called it the sin of articulation and prepared for meaning to
    defy me,
I loosed clamoring delirium, domesticated it.
I was once a fertile field of antique words,
I repaired a tomb, used treacherous sea-speech.
I shifted the shape of speech springing from books of slumber . . .
I broke through slumber,
chaotic night-dreams overflowing.
I unlocked the night, fraternized with my hand,
seducing the language of the body.
I mixed myself with waters of meaning.
Words flocked and whirled about my limbs.
Who will read this goblet, become enamored of my creatures . . .
    take wing?

Untitled

Vol. 2: 111

Standing on the sidewalk, waiting for a person
or a thing
I don't know him, he does not know me
he comes from behind
stabs me in the back
no motivation
before I breathe my last dream
I entreat him not to tell a soul.

If my life has been an open game
at least my death should remain a puzzle
this is the way I desire to die

The Citadel

Vol. 2: 168–69

This citadel
I build around me
stone by stone
summon
enemy armies
exhort them to fight
with appetite, with valor
with excellence in aiming
should they require grounds
to hone their weapons
I prepare them
I bait them with challenges
wait alone in my citadel
call every onslaught a seductive apple
no good at wars I detest weapons
own neither soldiers nor messengers
when they begin to retreat
I aid their wounded
send away war prisoners armed with gifts
build back the battered walls
paint them, decorate them
with lanterns
to guide their next attack
who knows? Perhaps at night
by myself I remain

so too the citadel.

Catalog of Suffering (Selections)

Vol. 2: 259–322

(1)
Taking off to translate the night . . .

(2)
If there is a lust within language, could we speak of it as the
 text's flesh? Its *body*?

(3)
Are you crying
for a nation? Or is
a nation crying for you?

Who are you?

You soaked the people with a teary elegy,
your desert girded with chieftains—
who are you?

Categorizing heavens with alarmed eyes,
uplifting our enemies with silence . . .
who are you?

(4)
Around him speech splinters,
mobilizes into battalions,
sets up, draws borders,
starts paralleling, pulling away,
surpassing, pouring out, the
primary text reduced to marginalia, footnotes
soon to be fire's lust.

None of this bothers him.
He's convinced he is the Text.

(5)
Write so our cry
rises.
Give the poem air,
venture some charged laments,
push us together . . . make us cry with you.
Your fancy will decide
just how to become our lamp
with your captivating madness.
Lead us into the darkness,
to words that do not end with sleep.
Write!
Master the form that yields to no form.

(6)
Night,
as if it were
the Night.

(7)
No scream of the flesh,
this corpse-madness,
this spirit-raving.

(8)
Amid tall grasses . . .
tyrants around him
armed to the molars with munitions.
He removes the flint's spark,
writes with it:
notebooks of fatigue,
descriptions of the prairie.

(9)
I read my blood,

as the night reads
the face
of this man called Qassim.

(10)
Flesh that dies with each desire,
born again with news of a ceasefire
between two deaths.
Flesh held taut, secure, by dykes,
inspected by passion,
I postponed the moment for your sake
using a pretext of manuscripts.
But here finally the body is going off to war,
no alphabet enough.

(11)
Hail, guardian of wine, peace be with you.
You go on about the history of grapes, then forget both grapes
and wine.
You bestow the ecstatic sway to our bodies.
When evening proceeds aflame
and the oil of our lamps is about to run dry,
you—in no genteel fashion—pour
an able-bodied vintage into bottles.

Lo, flames quit their slumber,
light flares to announce night's defeat.

(12)
Isolated, far away,
I examine the spirit's appeal,
the flesh's alchemy . . .

Arrives a voice racked with desire, refuting
physics,

a child who, inventing a dream,
slips into it.

(14)
What is hidden,
alarms.

(17)
I happened upon assassins at play
counting sacrificial victims in the ash of night,
praising God, denouncing the sins of Man.
Some of them untether the alphabet, spell names,
like scars on a corpse attacking the people.
Some repeat the number of victims
And their equivalence in earned pain.
Some honored themselves
hoping to deny death,
others stand captured within grave stupidity.

(18)
The forest people
ravage the house.

(20)
When people become bored with hunger's vainglory,
the gaiety of assassins gets outlandish.
They divide illusions:
victory here, defeat there.

Bodies racked with adrenaline and planned abandonment
stumble upon loot.

He departs with suppressed weeping.

No one attends to a person who's lost his crown
along with knightly valor.

He comes back,
captivated,

as if he'd been nowhere.

(21)
He said to them,
"There is a distance between me and the forest,
a distance between me and arms,
a distance between me and the herd.
There is a written text between me and God;
He does not infringe it, I do not violate it."
They were listening,
and seeing.

(22)
Only the sun
can imitate a sun.

(23)
As for you,
go ahead, feign sleep,
lose evening's appetite.

Only now you start shaking,
your eyes fixed upon the captivated beings
escaping into our dreams.

(25)
What a hairy little djinn you are!
You enjoy testing the most taut and proud of veins
while touching your hidden treasure,
ascending in suppressed sighs.
Why perch on a throne of haughtiness,
leaving your lover unattended,

trembling whenever he mentions a queen
who heaps up silver in the large, wooden bowl
of the body,
playing with gold gushing beneath her balcony?

(27)
They keep their braziers toasty.
You have only to thrust in your cold iron
to be properly skewered.

(29)
They call her the queen of djinn,
having slipped herself into a human robe.
Lifting the cloak over her head, she exchanges one nature
for another, her body
emerging from its night.

(30)
He was told:
You're being deceived, you lonely wolf.
Someone's meddling with your book,
tamping salt in the wound,
pushing you around
between illusion and dream.

He was told:
Best gather your fragments
unto your fragmented self,
decorate your den with cozy loneliness,
luxurious solitude.

He was told:
Get back to the cave's heart—
it holds more mercy for you
than love's illusion.

He was told:
Go find yourself.
That way you'll be sure no one can spoil your self
for you.
There . . . back to where you're alone,
go.

An impossible dream is kinder
than a rampaging ghost.

(32)
Alone,
within the night of the text,
creatures ooze into the howdah
of language.
He invents precious stones,
polished by sculptors
keeping vigil
on this discourse
of the text's flesh.

(33)
I saw in you the hidden paradise,
something water-like in your chemise;
a queen offering compassion to shepherds
in order to assault her subjects.

(34)
A crystal paradise.
Life outside it
is paradise.

(35)
Look, woman, my sobs like frightened lava
fly from my body.

Assert valor and wisdom
to believe in a day when
death can arrive with the calm
of grass
bleeding mud,
chance's ambiguity.

No time exists for you
to see where love lies
in life or in death.

(36)
Man, your child will beget children
who will sculpt a name for the body
and polish it with metals—
a body that neither ages nor weakens.

But wait! It's impaired, sick, perishing.
The spirit continues roving within groaning
bones. When the man dies,
hear the thump of the spirit
moving upward,
sounding like gold shattering
beneath the hooves of time.
Your child will beget children:
know that coming from books,
to books they will depart.

(37)
A child left alone at home
screams his throat dry—no one hears.
From the window a cloud covers him,
he stops his wailing, starts arranging pillows.
Night falls, dreams await him.

They weave a path from silken curtains
to distant depths.
Night descending, dreams awaiting.

(38)
A jungle,
or human beings?
Faces—eyes swaying
in the glass of space—
joy,
or a misery?

(39)
It was said that it is a body.
It was said that it is the inheritance of ancestors
overflowing to the ends of the sea,
ancestors saving a heritage that dams up the blood.
Also said: it is the ancient stone
gushing forth in glass polished
by suspirations:
a body writing one body,
read by another body.

(40)
My insides ached for you,
my blood craved you,
my heart is weeping like the planets.

(60)
His lust for mirrors tapers off,
quicksilver chatter proving a bore.

(61)
For her, his version of life:
"Sliver of light betwixt two nights."

(65)
Here is a book for you,
read to you.

(74)
We come out of a dying cave's
        Darkness,
The end much
As it began:
Life voyage of a bird
        and a spider.

(79)
What the Night said about him:
"Handsome,
Like a stranger entering a house, igniting it with light."

(84)
On him the dictionaries poured their diffuse essences.
Opening a window, he raised his wings
and sang unto the nebulae:
"This is the goblet untying our tongues."

(104)
Whenever my friends amuse themselves
        with my wounds
I am on the road
        to death.

(111)
Gold's memory bequeaths to iron
the secrets of alchemy
and advises forgetting the future.

(112)
He described the night, saying,

Life filled with justifications
        for regret,
if it were to recur
        I would not flee
would not spare a single regret.

(114)
Alarmed, he fell back, alone, to the cave,
        Sobbing,
"That which is love they call
        Slaying."

(119)
To the speech of a rock
ablaze beside the abyss,
in rapture
I listen.

(121)
A mountain goat—wind defeating his horns—
makes light
of a mountain rock.

(122)
He told life about death:
"Confront the world.
At the same time
show it your back."

(125)
They race,
his end
and the text's last word:
What will our progeny do

with this manuscript of hope,
this unfinished book?

(129)
I came.
I came
and no one
was there.

(134)
Grudges flourish
when the hugs
are most tight.

(138)
Whenever he opens a book
he reads another name into his name,
shared by dictionaries
he will one day
be owned by lexicons.

(139)
He retires,
        renounces war.
Still it comes
        always it comes.

(140)
He bade farewell to friends
dying with a grudge
once the sirens of sleep
caught up with his soul.

(142)
I have died from time to time.

(143)
I master no map,
am neither traveler nor resident,
places are so many chains
        tightened,
polished by my comings
and goings.

(145)
He who rubbed his two wrists
on night's rock—
how can he forget?

(146)
With words he furnishes the grave,
as a man
might sing
wedding songs
to himself.

(147)
To see the text with his heart
he shuts his eyes
as if praying:
"O Death . . .
my Beloved"

(149)
No death
just absence
persisting.

(150)
People fear in me
ugliness made manifest

while, in them, I shrink
from the latent.

(151)
Worn to near nothing,
he sleeps beneath his skin
like a sheet
stretched
to accommodate dreams.

(152)
Just opening a window onto water
sets my language on fire
like a chemise weeping for a body.

(154)
I moved my soul from the body
to the margin
of the text
and prepared it for possible
absence
as if the book
would grant me
its ranging fire.

(155)
He says to us (but more to himself):
"The loser loses nothing."

(158)
Forgetting does not suffice:
Not possible
to reclaim them.

(160)
Time for the author

to grant the text
its desires
time for the soul to expire.

He Was Told: O Muhammad

Vol. 2: 435–38

He was dreaming
half in water
half braiding a rope,
between them lay an air placenta.
The two halves write on wood what salt and fish bones erase.
He carries the wind under his arms, dandling the sails
so he doesn't miss the horizon.

In that state of blissful fatigue
between journeying and full rest
hearing seashells while the nature of absence listened to him
his heart homebound
he was told,
O Muhammad, this is your naughty child.
Forgive him for his past and coming misdeeds
your child who sleeps when people go to work
with hearts honed by obdurate sadness
he sobs
your child—yours for better or worse—
shoves his allure between the rose and the garden
                              between the word and the
                              meaning
opens the horizon to an abyss of allusions
with diligent caring
so he was told.

In the iron smithy
his ragged shirt released from sails
revealing more than shielding
he is hit by regrets of departure and homecoming tears,

between him and water lies extinguished camaraderie
between him and fire lies the kindled yearning.
He takes half the earth as his *izar*
while his chest is in the winds
                    in the flying fragments
iron fetters on his anklebone
and a chain on his back
his Khadija on the spindle of time
neither losing nor possessing him.

O Muhammad, he is your child.
You see him as you seize iron succumbing to the flame's desire.
O Muhammad:
Show him mercy
say not *uf*! in anger
chide him not
he, the child who offered you the wing of humility
carried the sack of your bones
proclaimed you like a banner among tribes.
With your body he circumambulated
washing away the fields' oil
charging your body with dates and milk.

He was told . . .
in his late childhood he was a cradle
rocked by God's hand
seagulls hankering over him
reciting the sea message—
a child growing old and aging
overrun by the silver of sleep.
His dreams vouch for him
between his hands palm trees grow
a nightly paradise

all contained . . .
his son has no power over him.

O Muhammad
ravings afflict you
iron possesses you
tremors of the remotest take hold of you
so whirl around as you desire
betake yourself by inspiration as you desire
you have the right to be misled by your son
as he disobeys, repudiates, goes astray
leading a rebellion against you.

He was told: O Muhammad
your child is like you
he inherited your silence, your solitude, your caverns
he glorifies you and becomes weary of you
he was told, O Muhammad . . .
but he was in the iron grip of the dream.

Love

Daʿ al-Malak: 35

The poetry you write
hones love in your soul
you become light, transparent
akin to crystal.

You go to your sleep: a master of the treasure, of writing.

If you don't conceive such love in your poetry
in your small matter,
in the movement of your body,
in the garden of your soul,
in the sap masked in mirrors,
how can you claim to us
that you make this moment of beauty for others?

The Hermit's Spindle

Da' al-Malak: 37–38

Soft like silk that veils the face,
making angels' fingers sense
and harken back to a bed brimming
with dreams.

Do you know it?
Rain with the grace of a spindle
whose tearful fall in slumber's glass
defies perception.
Steps flow
from the tail ends of a cloud clinging to air tips
to keep from falling.

They fall in the galaxy of your roving, preoccupied body—
rain being the medium.

Rain itself
will waken the light of your slumbering wickets
rain
silk

counts the bottles at the peak of crimson disclosures
while they reel from an excess of wine.

Appendix

✖

Explanatory Notes

Provisions for Mere Survival: A Kiss on the Forehead— Paradise Recalled

Qassim Haddad, *Warshat al-Amal*. Muharraq, Bahrain: Markaz al-Shaykh Ibrahim Al Khalifa, 2004. 129–35.

An early lesson, whose details persist, came to me in the form of a gesture. This image, one and the same as my desire to recall childhood, has been so abridged that I'm not sure if I was ever a child at any given moment or whether my childhood was a dream.

I grew up in a household where all family members worked continuously at varied jobs; their work barely allowed for subsistence. In that period (around 1950), the work in Bahrain was hard and the money minimal. A destitute society was moving away from pearl diving. Diving was not much different from *corvée* labor; this complex exploitation turned boatmen into the equivalent of slaves. As soon as the poor moved out from relying on pearl-diving illusions, they fell into oil illusions, which put them in the grip of a new exploitation. Merchants and oil companies worked to extract, simultaneously, the blood of the workers and the oil from the fields. This led to quickly shaping, developing, and accentuating popular sentiments of anger that in turn led to widespread popular struggles. These struggles have stormed Bahrain and the surrounding area since the beginning of the 1940s. During these transformations, the working classes were always candidates for great suffering that led families of this stratum to search for modes of living in any legitimate way that existed. This is what made us come across the phenomenon of having all members of the family engaged in work—not only men, young men, and boys, but also and especially women.

Around seven years old, I became aware of this life surrounding me and recall my father repeating a common saying when he described his daily efforts to make ends meet. In such a setting, he said that only the popular and widely known proverbial saying, *qut la tamut*, summed things up: "provisions for mere survival." He added vaguely, "They (assuming we knew who he meant) want exactly this for us—this, nothing more or less. They want us to surrender to our work as slaves do. At the same time, they don't want us dying from starvation. As a result, we persist on the border of life and death."

My father repeated this saying as if he were shielding himself and training us for harsher times. He experimented with work of all kinds—from those associated with the sea to those having to do with iron. Alongside him, the other family men labored—each to his liking and professional skill. The women in the family also worked day and night, both inside the house and out. They made up ways to extract a bit of extra income. One should not minimize the role of women in confronting *"qut la tamut."* At times, their work would determine our survival, especially when the men couldn't find work and sat at home like lions waiting for ready-made prey.

Still very young, I watched the yard of the big family house turn into a beehive from dawn till dusk. In a pen inside the house, my grandmother had two cows that produced milk, and all the foods that come from milk. One of my aunts embroidered women's clothing with golden straw. She used special embroidery handtools on a wooden hoop over which a piece of fabric was stretched. Late into the night my aunt would stay working over this hoop. My other aunt worked here and there for neighborhood women, earning next to nothing. In one household, she helped stitch by hand the golden floss on cloaks and dresses (called *kurar*); in another house, she did the laundry. My mother knew how to work a traditional sewing machine and sewed clothes for neighborhood folk, collecting a precious few dirhams. After about three years of schooling, my sister started helping her sew.

In this workshop dedicated to securing provisions for survival, many things were considered unnecessary; in fact, some things were considered luxuries not even to be thought of. At times, under pressure, the family even gave up some of the necessities. But how could a child of seven recognize, without a shocking jolt, the notion of luxury under the conditions of *qut la tamut*?

I remember days when the family found itself, without acknowledging it, sharing the fodder of my grandmother's cows. This took place with a measure of innocence—the innocence of the poor—as if it were a normal thing. Possibly it was due to the dynamic relations between the members of my family and the benevolent cows. When the fodder sacks—made of date pits—were brought home to spread out so we could separate the fodder from the dirt, we would find some dry dates along with the pits. We collected these dates, washed them, then my grandmother roasted them with the leftover, melted cow butter. This provided us with a nutritive and delicious meal that my father and uncle shared with us in a jolly, memorable ambiance. All this led to turning the arrival of the cows' fodder into a family occasion charged with pleasure.

These scenes formed a comprehensive lesson that my memory wouldn't dismiss. But the personal lesson that I am about to relate happened when waiting for the return of my father on a critical day.

I was in the second grade. Coming home, I went directly to my father, stating my wish to exchange my cheap, worn sandals for white shoes like the ones my school friends had. My father's day had been so difficult to handle that hearing his pampered and only son ask for new white shoes was the last straw. For me, the request symbolized a monumental transition from the age of sandals to the age of shoes—an event worthy of note. The problem was my timing. Only later did I discover that fact. Traumatized, my father had been searching all day for work, in vain. As well, he was being pressed to pay a debt from his pearl-diving days. Both these things were coming at a time when family provisions had practically run out. In short, I was putting salt on his wounds, doubling his agony.

The child was shocked by the explosion of the volcano between his hands as his father thundered—his scream rattling in the house as if he were appealing to the heavens to save him from such unbearable suffering. Given my shock, I could not recognize another reason—apart from me—for my father's explosion. Frightened, I ran to my mother who took me in her lap, having grasped what was going on. Everyone expected that my father's anger, as usual, would soon—in a matter of moments—turn into a soft breeze. That day's anger was different. It was a day that needed a night replete with sentiments demonstrating love to be more solid than life itself, and made my lesson's significance complete.

By midnight, the large family began to calm down, were lying on their beds, anxiety reigning in every room. I was in the small room—my father alone on a modest bed, my mother, elder sister, and I on the floor. I was not sleepy at all. I felt as if I could hear the heartbeats of my father and the fast throbs of arteries in the blazing heart of my mother's chest. All of a sudden, I heard the movement of my mother in the depth of darkness as she opened her small chest under my father's bed and crawled to his head whispering, as if imploring. I gradually gathered she was passing on to him some money that she had collected from her work as a seamstress so that he could take me the next day to the market place and buy me the shoes I wanted.

"He is our only son; we are used to poverty, but do not break the heart of your son, O Muhammad."

O Muhammad!

Before that night, I had never heard my mother address my father by his first name. For the first time, I witnessed the relation between my parents clearly, directly, rigorously, and lovingly, all in a moment. I had to close my ears in order not to hear the tense and fast beating throbs of my father's heart. His words were like a sob as he stammered out some vague statement. As if to engrave this moment in my memory, my father could not sleep before coming close to me, thinking I was fast asleep. He brushed my face with a kiss that I fancied was paradise.

And as if all this was not enough—

The lesson was to be completed in the morning when his two sisters who had collected a sum from their humble income and added more to it from grandmother's old box surprised my father. They handed it to him so that the house's only son could get the white shoes he desired.

The lesson was painfully significant. For the first time, I felt that my enrolling in school would be a burden for the family by doubling our living expenses. I say it was a painfully significant lesson because in fact from then on I came to have an undeclared grudge towards schooling.

Was I expressing the sufficiency of this early, cruel lesson in order to avoid other lessons?

From that day, I unconsciously prepared myself to engage in practical life without lingering in a period of ambivalent childhood or abridged youth. I found myself in the midst of life's serious demands. Accordingly I started helping to shoulder my father's burden, trying my best to understand the meaning of going beyond the harsh popular saying, *qut la tamut.*

Explanatory Notes

Introduction

Akhbar Majnun Layla is the title of this cycle of poems around the well-known legend of Qays, who was known as Majnun Layla—the Madman of Layla—so enamored of his beloved that he was named after her. The crucial term in the title that resists easy rendering in English is *Akhbar*, plural of *khabar*. *Khabar* suggests a report that is factual, narrated, and disseminated through oral transmission. Since this collection is in verse, one can call it a narrative poem. But this does not cancel the factual and historical dimension of *khabar*. Haddad, like many poets before him, is rewriting the historical legend, embellishing it, restructuring it, or adapting it.

Chronicles of Majnun Layla

qasida (p. 18) stands for a poem. In its classical use, it stood for an elaborate poem comparable to the ode. Based on one single meter and characterized by monorhyme and two hemistiches, it addressed various themes.

Qays (p. 18) is identified in Arabic lore with different names. The most dominant of them is Qays ibn al-Mulawwah.

Abu Bakr al-Walibi (p. 19) is an ambiguous figure in literary Arabic literature; he is said to have collected the poetry of Majnun Layla. Very little is known about his life. Abu Faraj al-Asfahani (897–967) is the author of *Kitab al-Aghani* (The Book of Songs), a multivolume work of literary history and of sung poetry.

oral transmitters (p. 19) refers to a chain of transmitters in order to authenticate the actuality of an incident or a saying that is communicated orally (X said according to Y who heard it from Z, etc.). The chain of transmitting knowledge (known as *isnad*) is often used to establish the authenticity of an oral text, but in this case it is used ironically to raise doubts as to the authenticity of information about Majnun Layla.

fatwa (p. 20) is a juridical ruling based on interpretation of Islamic law.

"East wind of Najd . . ." (p. 20) is a verse line from a classical poem and is used here intertextually to express yearning and longing for the location of the beloved.

siwak-**tree** (p. 25) is *Salvadore persica*, a plant found in Arabia. Its twigs are used to clean the teeth.

kufiyya (p. 25) is a traditional headdress worn by men.

'Amma yatasa'lun (p. 26) is a Quranic section of several short chapters that is often recited and memorized. It starts with the verse *'amma yatasa'lun* ("Of what do they question one another?")—the opening verse of Surat al-Naba' (chapter 78, "The Tiding")—and thus is named after it.

Dhu al-Hijja (p. 28) is the last month in the lunar Islamic calendar. It is the month in which the hajj (pilgrimage) to Mecca takes place coinciding with Eid al-Adha (the Sacrifice Feast).

Kaaba (p. 28) is the Noble Cube in the Holy Mosque of Mecca. Muslims orient themselves towards it when they pray. It is the central destination of pilgrims.

kohl (p. 29) is an eye cosmetic made by grinding natural ingredients. Its use has long been widespread in Asia and Africa.

haram (p. 43) is Arabic for unlawful or forbidden.

she-ass (p. 45) as an allegorical reference to Layla might be a biblical allusion related to Christ entering Jerusalem on a she-ass.

Safa and **Marwa** (p. 46) are elevated sites in Mecca. Muslims travel between them seven times during hajj as part of the religious ritual.

Mount Tawbad (p. 47) is situated in Najd in the Arabian peninsula in the area where Layla is supposed to have lived.

shari'a (p. 57) is Islamic principles and rules of law.

Marwan Ibn al-Hakam (623–685) (p. 59) is the fourth Umayyad caliph.

Ibn Jawziyya (1292–1350) (p. 62) was a prolific Islamic jurist and theologian.

halal (p. 63) is that which is permissible in Islamic law.

Kalam ibn Wahsh (p. 64) is a fictional jurist.

faqih (p. 64) is an Islamic scholar who specializes in jurisprudence.

legalized shedding of blood (p. 72) refers to a tribal custom where some-one who has broken the law of the tribe can be put to death (i.e., have his blood shed) by anyone.

"Tell Us, O Scheherazade"

Scheherazade (p. 80) is the protagonist in *The Arabian Nights,* condemned to execution at dawn. She tells stories to Sultan Shahrayar at night to delay her death verdict. Her tales that captivate the sultan go on for 1,001 nights after which she is pardoned.

abaya (p. 80) is a body-covering cloak worn by traditional Middle East-ern women in public.

hulu (p. 81) is a pearl-diving chant.

thawb (p. 81) is a traditional formal dress worn by women in the Arabian Gulf.

"Alphabet of the Arab Twentieth Century: *Alif*"

Alif (p. 83) is the first letter in the Arabic alphabet.

"Love Feast"

Carmathians (p. 93) were a Shi'ite group that revolted against the Abassid caliphate in the late ninth century and tried to establish an ideal republic. Bahrain was one of their strongholds.

"Untitled"

This poem (p. 102) is an epigraph to the collection *'Izlat al-Malikat* (Isolation of Queens).

Catalog of Suffering (poem 32)

howdah (p. 110) is a seat with a canopy placed on the back of a camel and used as means of transportation particularly for women. It is an Anglicization of the Arabic word *howdaj*.

"He Was Told: O Muhammad"

izar (p. 120) is a traditional Arab wrap clothing that resembles a sarong.

Khadija (p. 120) is the name of Qassim's mother and the wife of Muhammad his father who is apostrophized in the poem. It is also the quintessential name for a woman in the Arab world.

uf! (p. 120) is an exclamation that indicates one has had enough.

Other titles in Middle East Literature in Translation

Abundance from the Desert: Classical Arabic Poetry
    Raymond Farrin

Beyond Love
    Hadiya Hussein; Ikram Masmoudi, trans.

Canceled Memories: A Novel
    Nazik Saba Yared

Contemporary Iraqi Fiction: An Anthology
    Shakir Mustafa, trans. and ed.

The Emperor Tea Garden
    Nazlı Eray

A Muslim Suicide
    Bensalem Himmich; Roger Allen, trans.

My Bird
    Fariba Vafi; Mahnaz Kousha and Nasrin Jewell, trans.

Thou Shalt Not Speak My Language
    Abdelfattah Kilito; Waïl S. Hassan, trans.

Tree of Pearls, Queen of Egypt
    Jurji Zaydan

The Virgin of Solitude: A Novel
    Taghi Modarressi; Nasrin Rahimieh, trans.